THE ROBIN HOOD STORIES

WEBSTER EVERYREADERS

ROBIN HOOD STORIES

KING ARTHUR AND HIS KNIGHTS

THE TROJAN WAR

GREEK AND ROMAN MYTHS

ON JUNGLE TRAILS

INDIAN PAINT

WILD ANIMALS I HAVE KNOWN

BOB, SON OF BATTLE

THE CALL OF THE WILD

THE GOLD BUG AND OTHER STORIES

CASES OF SHERLOCK HOLMES

IVANHOE

THE FLAMINGO FEATHER

MEN OF IRON

BEN HUR

JUAREZ, HERO OF MEXICO

TO HAVE AND TO HOLD

THE SILVER SKATES

TREASURE ISLAND

KIDNAPPED

The Robin Hood Stories

Adapted by William Kottmeyer
St. Louis Public Schools
Illustrated by JAMES CUMMINS

WEBSTER DIVISION, McGRAW-HILL BOOK COMPANY
St. Louis New York San Francisco Dallas Toronto London Sydney

The Webster Everyreaders

The EVERYREADERS were selected from the great literature of the world and adapted to the needs of today's children. This series retains the flavor of the originals, providing mature content and dramatic plot structure, along with eye appeal designed to motivate reading.

This approach was first developed in the renowned St. Louis Reading Clinic by Dr. Kottmeyer and is the direct outgrowth of wide and successful teaching of remedial reading.

A high interest level plus the carefully controlled vocabulary and sentence structure enable pupils to read the stories easily, confidently, and with enjoyment.

Seventeenth Printing, 1972.

Copyright 1952 by McGraw-Hill, Inc. All Rights Reserved. Printed in the United States of America. This book, or parts thereof, may not be reproduced in any form without permission of the publishers.

Copyright in Great Britain and in the British Dominions and Possessions.

ISBN 07-033731-4

Contents

The Robin Hood Stories.................... 1

Robin Becomes an Outlaw.................. 5

The Sheriff's Shooting Match............... 9

Robin Hood Meets Little John.............. 19

How Robin and His Men Saved Will Stutely.... 27

Little John Meets His Match................ 35

Robin Hood Meets Will Scarlet............. 43

Allan-a-Dale Comes to Sherwood Forest........ 53

Robin Hood Finds Friar Tuck................ 61

Robin Hood Goes to a Wedding.............. 73

Robin Hood Helps a Sad Knight.............. 81

How Sir Richard of the Lea Paid What He Owed 97

Robin Hood Shoots for the Queen............103

The King's Men Chase Robin................117

Robin Hood Fights Guy of Gisborn............127

King Richard Comes to Sherwood Forest......141

The Robin Hood Stories

In England's Sherwood Forest long ago there lived a band of famous outlaws. Now Sherwood Forest was the King's forest. No man could hunt the deer or other animals. Those were for the king and his rich friends. The king's woodsmen guarded the woods. Any man who shot a deer lost his head — if the king's men caught him.

But the outlaws were afraid of nobody. They knew the woods and could easily get away from the King's men. They dressed in green clothes which were hard to see against the green leaves. They were great shots with the bow and arrow. They could swing a sword with the best fighters in

England. Day after day they practiced fighting with long poles called cudgels.

The rich people hated the outlaws. When they came through Sherwood Forest, the outlaws were sure to rob them. Bitter enemies of the outlaws were the Sheriff of Nottingham and the Bishop of Hereford. Again and again they tried to catch the clever outlaws.

But the poor people loved the robbers. The money the outlaws took from the rich they gave to the poor. They kept little for themselves. They never killed unless somebody tried to kill them. They never hurt a woman or child.

Leader of the outlaws was Robin Hood. No man could shoot the long bow like Robin Hood. Few men could stand up to him with sword or cudgel. Kind and wise, he led the outlaws against their enemies.

The old stories say his real name was Robert Fitzooth. Robert was born in Locksley, near Sherwood Forest. Some say his father, Hugh Fitzooth, was cheated out of his money and castle. So the father became a woodsman. But still his enemies would not let him alone. They had him thrown into prison. His wife, left with little Robert, got sick and died. The news came to the father, and a little later he died, too.

The boy, Robert, went to live with his uncle, George Gamewell. There he grew up with his cousin, Will Gamewell.

But soon Robert was left alone with his uncle. Will went off to school. Robert, now called Robin, spent most of his time in the woods. There he practiced with bow and arrow until he was a good shot.

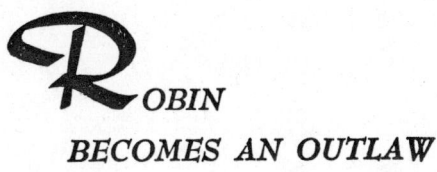

ROBIN BECOMES AN OUTLAW

When Robin was eighteen, the Sheriff of Nottingham held a great shooting match.

"We shall see," he said, "who shoots the best around Nottingham. Get the best men you can find. We shall give a rich prize to the winner."

The news spread. When Robin heard about it, he wanted to go.

"Uncle," he said, "I'd like to get in that match. Do you think I'd have a chance?"

"Why not go?" said his uncle. "You're just a boy, but you're a good shot. Try it."

"I'll do it," said Robin. He took up his bow and his best arrows. Then he started off through Sherwood Forest. Nottingham lay just on the other side of the woods.

Suddenly he came upon a small band of men lying under an oak tree. They were eating and drinking and having a good time. Robin stopped. They were the king's woodsmen.

"Look who's here," called one. "Isn't he a pretty boy? And he's got his little bow and arrow! Where are you going, boy?"

Robin looked at him angrily.

"My bow is as good as yours," he said. "I'm going to the Sheriff's shooting match."

"Ha!" laughed another. "Do you think you can shoot with men? I'll bet you can't even pull that bow string back."

"Is that so?" said Robin. "I can shoot as well as any of you."

Everybody laughed.

"You can brag when you cannot prove it," said the first man.

"No?" said Robin. "Look over there. See those deer down there? I'll bet I can hit that big one in the middle. Why don't you step up and shoot, too? I'll bet you twenty silver coins that I hit him."

"That's a bet," cried the man. "Twenty silver coins say you can't. Go on and shoot." He jumped to his feet and picked up his bow.

Now Robin put the string on his bow. He picked out a good arrow. He pulled the feather back to his ear. The arrow flashed through the trees. The big deer leaped high into the air and fell dead. The red blood ran on the grass. Everybody held his breath. It was a wonderful shot. Then Robin spoke:

"How do you like that? Pay me."

"Silver?" cried the man. "You'd better get out of here — and fast. Don't you know you shot the king's deer?"

"Let's take him in," said another.

"No," said a third. "He's just a boy. Let him go. Come, boy, get out of here."

Robin saw they did not mean to pay the bet. He walked off without a word.

But the man who had made the bet was still angry. He watched Robin walk away. Suddenly he put an arrow into his bow. He took quick aim and sent the arrow at

Robin's back. It flew past Robin, barely missing him. Robin jumped.

"You still don't think I can shoot, do you?" he cried. He pulled back the string. The arrow came flying straight. The forester dropped, shot through the heart. Robin ran. The others did not dare chase him.

But, as he ran, Robin knew he had killed a man — the king's man. He could never go back to his uncle's home. Before night a reward was out for him. Robin was an outlaw.

Now Sherwood Forest became his home. One by one, men in trouble came to stay with him. At last more than a hundred men were with him. They chose him to be their leader and called him Robin Hood. Because they helped the poor, the people grew to love them. The outlaws never hurt children or women, so they did not fear him or his men. But the Sheriff of Nottingham said he would get him. He wanted the reward — and the honor of catching the famous outlaw.

THE SHERIFF'S SHOOTING MATCH

The Sheriff sent his men into Sherwood Forest again and again. But never could they catch Robin Hood and his men. The Nottingham people began to joke about it. This made the Sheriff still more angry.

"Why can't you catch him?" he cried. His men just looked at him.

"He knows the forest too well," said one. "He can keep out of our way. We have to stay together. If we spread out, he'll catch us instead. We need more men."

"More men? Where can I get more men?" cried the Sheriff. "If the king knew this —" He stopped. "The king! That's it! I'll go to London myself. King Henry will help me. Get ready, everybody. We'll go to London. I'll have that Robin Hood yet!"

The Sheriff's men shined their armor and cleaned their swords. In a few days they were on the way to London. There King Henry and Queen Elinor had their court. The Sheriff and his men were taken in to the king and queen.

"My Lord," said the Sheriff kneeling, "I come to ask help."

"Help?" smiled the King. "What kind of help?"

"My lord, you know Sherwood Forest well. There lives an outlaw named Robin Hood. I have tried to catch him, but he always gets away."

"Ah, yes," said the King. "We have heard of him. Some say he is a good man."

"He shoots your deer. He robs the rich people who go through Sherwood."

The King began to get angry.

"He does, does he? And who is sheriff there? What is a sheriff for? Here you come with all these men. What do you want me to do about it? You see that my laws are obeyed. If you can't, I'll get another sheriff. Now, get out."

"But, my lord —"

"No more! Get out!"

So the Sheriff and his men rode sadly home. The Sheriff spoke to no one. He was busy thinking.

"I've got it!" cried the Sheriff. "I know how to get him."

"How?" cried his men.

"If I can get him into Nottingham we can catch him."

"How shall we get him there?"

"You know he's a great shot with bow and arrow. Now what if I'd have a big shooting match in Nottingham? What if I would give a fine prize to the winner? Don't you think he would get into the match?"

"I know him," said one. "If there's a shooting match, he'll be there."

"But don't think he will walk into our hands," said another.

"He won't be wearing green," said a third.

"No," said the Sheriff, "but many of you have seen him before. He has long yellow hair. We can tell when he comes. Then I'll give the word. You all get near him. We'll throw him into jail and then we'll hang him."

Soon everybody was talking about the grand shooting match. The best shots for miles around were getting ready. The prize was to be a golden arrow. Robin and his men soon heard about the match.

"Men," said Robin, "I think we should have that arrow. One of us can win it. Wouldn't the Sheriff be angry if we did?"

"I don't like this," said an outlaw. "I heard people talk at Nottingham. They say the Sheriff is having this shooting match just to catch you. He's waiting for you to come. When you're there they'll jump you. I'm against it."

Robin laughed. "I've heard that too. But is the Sheriff going to scare us away? Do you want everyone to say we were afraid to come?"

"No, but I don't want to see you hang."

"You won't," said Robin. "I'm going to shoot for that arrow. Here is our plan. You men wear old clothes. Take your swords. Spread out through the crowd. See that no one can tell who you are. If something goes wrong, you will all be there."

The match was held just outside Nottingham. Along the wall were seats for the rich people. Near the target was a place for the Sheriff and his wife. On the other side was a low fence. Here the poor people could stand to watch the shooting.

The crowd came early. Slowly the seats for the rich people began to fill. At last the Sheriff and his wife came, riding their horses.

When the Sheriff had sat down, he told his man to blow the horn. Now the men who were to shoot came forward. The Sheriff gave them the rules:

"The target is 150 yards away. Everybody shoots from that line. Each man shoots one arrow. The ten best shots shoot again; the others drop out. Each of the three winners shoots three arrows. The best shot wins the golden arrow."

The men began to shoot. As each man shot, the Sheriff and his men looked him over.

"Could that be Robin Hood?" he asked again and again.

But none was sure. Not one archer wore the green suit Robin's men wore.

"Let's wait," said the Sheriff. "When there are only ten left it will be easier. If he's here, he'll be one of the ten."

Cheer after cheer rose from the people. Never had the people seen such good shooting. At last only ten men were left. Most of them were famous. Two came from a nearby town. Another was a big man in blue from London. The last one was a stranger in an old red suit. He wore a patch over one eye.

"Now," said the Sheriff to his men, "look at them. Is Robin Hood one of them?"

The Sheriff's men scratched their heads.

"You know those first ones as well as we, my lord," said one. "One of those two strangers is too tall. The other is too short."

"That's right," said another. "And Robin is broader than the tall man in blue."

"How about that man in red?"

"He's about the right size, but Robin has yellow hair. You can see that man's hair is brown."

"Then he is afraid," cried the Sheriff. "He was afraid to come."

The ten men now shot their arrows. The three best were Gilbert Red Cap, a second man, and the strange man in red. The people cheered.

"Now, Gilbert," called the Sheriff, "you are my man. Go on and win."

"I'm going to," said Gilbert. He put his arrow to his bow carefully. He stepped to the mark and aimed. He let it go. The arrow landed almost in the center.

"A good shot, Gilbert!" cried the Sheriff. Again the crowd cheered. Now the stranger in red stepped forward. He put an arrow to his bow, raised it, and let it fly.

Whack! The flying arrow cut a piece off

Gilbert's arrow and hit the center. The shot was a bull's eye! The third man put his arrow away.

"I quit," he said. "I can't beat that."

Almost without aiming, the stranger now quickly shot two more arrows. Both hit the center of the target. His three arrows looked like one big one.

Well, there was nothing to do but give the stranger the prize. The Sheriff was angry because Gilbert had lost.

"Here," he said, "you win the arrow. Who are you? Where are you from?"

The stranger leaned on his bow. He looked the Sheriff up and down.

"I'm Rob Locksley, from Locksley Town."

"Well, Rob, you are the best shot I ever saw. How would you like to work for me? I'll give you better clothes than those. You'll get the best to eat and drink. I'll pay you good money. What do you say?"

"No," said the stranger. "I'm my own boss and I like it. I work for nobody."

"Then take your prize and get out," cried the Sheriff. He threw the arrow to the stranger. Then he turned and walked off. The stranger caught the arrow and laughed. In a minute he was gone.

Later that day strangely dressed men hurried through Sherwood Forest. When they met, they took off their strange clothes. Underneath were suits of Lincoln green. They laughed and talked about the great Nottingham shooting match.

One man pulled off his old red suit. Then he took off the patch over his eye. He put his hand to his hair.

"I won't get this brown color out of my hair very soon," said Robin Hood. "But I guess this was worth it." He held up the Sheriff's golden arrow. The men cheered.

"I could hardly keep from laughing," said an outlaw. "There you were, close enough to touch him. What if he knew?"

"And then he wanted you to work for him," laughed another. "It's too bad he doesn't know the truth."

"Men," said Robin, "I think he ought to know, don't you?"

"He should! He should!"

"Then he shall," said Robin with a smile.

That evening the Sheriff had a great dinner in Nottingham. The Sheriff and his friends sat in the great hall eating. Everybody was still talking about the match.

"I did think Robin Hood would be there today," said the Sheriff. "But he must have been afraid to come. Well, I'm glad to know he was afraid."

"I wonder where that one-eyed man in red went," said one. "Rob Locksley! I never heard of him before. He could shoot!"

"I should have thrown him into jail," said the Sheriff.

Just then something flashed over their heads. An arrow, flying through an open window, stuck in the wall. A piece of paper was wrapped around it.

Pale and shaking, the Sheriff unrolled it. On the inside he read these words:

Thanks for the golden arrow,
Dear Sheriff, kind and good.
The stranger dressed in dirty red
Was your old friend,
    Robin Hood

ROBIN HOOD MEETS LITTLE JOHN

One morning Robin Hood got up bright and early.

"Boys," he said, "things have been pretty quiet here. I'm going out alone today. Don't get too far away. If I need you, I'll give you the signal — I'll blow my horn three times."

"We'll be there when you need us," said Will Stutely. The other outlaws nodded.

So Robin walked off through the woods. He went along a brook. Soon he came to a log lying across the water. He stepped on the log to cross to the other side. But as he looked up, he saw someone else coming to his side. It was a tall stranger, bigger than any man Robin had ever seen. They got to the middle of the little bridge almost together. Both stopped.

"Well?" said Robin.

"Well?" said the stranger.

"Get back to your side," said Robin. "I'm coming over."

"Get back yourself. I started over first. The better man is going to cross first. Get out of his way."

"We will see about that," said Robin. "How would you like to run into a fast arrow?"

"You touch an arrow and I'll pound you with this cudgel."

"Don't be silly," said Robin. "I can put an arrow between your ribs before you lift that cudgel."

"My, you're brave," said the stranger. "I have no bow, so you want to fight with bows."

"Why," said Robin, "I'll fight you any way you want." He threw his bow and arrows on the bank. Then he walked over and cut himself a strong cudgel. The

stranger stayed on the bridge and waited.

"Ready?" asked Robin.

"Ready," said the stranger.

Robin looked him over carefully. He saw a man fully seven feet tall. Robin himself had broad shoulders, but this man was even broader.

"You're pretty big," he said, "but you're going to get a beating. We'll stand on this bridge. We fight until one man gets knocked into the water."

"That's fine," said the stranger.

He swung his cudgel. Had the blow landed, it would have laid Robin flat. Quick as a flash he ducked. He hit out with his own cudgel at the stranger's ribs. Whack! The stranger knocked Robin's cudgel aside. Again he swung, but Robin was too quick for him. Try as he would, Robin could not hit him. Robin was quicker, but the stranger was stronger. The fight grew hotter. They fought for almost an hour. Each man still kept his place on the bridge.

After a while they rested. Then they went at it again. The big stranger was puffing hard now. But Robin, too, was getting tired. Never, he thought, had he seen a fighter like this one. Then Robin suddenly saw his chance. He hit the stranger hard in his ribs. The big man grunted. Over he leaned, almost falling. Robin was sure he had him. But the stranger kept on his feet. At the same time he swung. The big cudgel caught Robin just over his ear. His feet flew into the air. He hit the water with a great splash.

The cold water brought him to quickly. He spit out water and looked up. The big stranger was standing on the bridge laughing.

"Who is the better man?" he cried.

Robin's head still hurt, but he had to laugh, too. He reached up his hand.

"Help me up," he said. The stranger pulled him up as if he were a baby.

"Well," said Robin, "you're the best man I ever saw." He put his horn to his lips. He blew three times. The stranger looked at him in surprise. In a few minutes Robin's men ran out of the woods.

"Master!" cried Will Stutely. "What is the matter? You're all wet."

"Why," laughed Robin, "this big fellow just knocked me into the water. No wonder I'm wet."

"He did?" cried Will. "Let's give him a drink then, too. Come on, men."

Will and the others jumped on the stranger. He knocked two or three down, but they soon had him.

"No, no!" laughed Robin. "He's a good man. He beat me in a fair fight. Stranger, I like you. How would you like to be one of us? It's a free life and an easy one. If you do, you shall be my right-hand man."

But the stranger was still angry. Two men were still sitting on his chest. The others held his arms and legs.

"Oh, I don't know," he said. "I beat you with a cudgel. I think I can beat you at anything. I think I can shoot better, too. I'll tell you. If you can beat me with bow and arrow, I'll be one of your men."

"All right," said Robin. "But you don't have to come with us. I'll show you you can't beat me, though. Will Stutely, set up a target."

Will cut a piece of white wood as big as his hand. He walked about seventy-five yards and put it on a tree.

"Now, stranger," said Robin, "let us see you hit it."

"Give me a strong bow and a good arrow."

Somebody gave him his bow. The stranger picked out an arrow. He aimed carefully. Straight down the path flew the arrow. It hit the target in the center. The stranger stepped back.

"Beat that!" he said.

"Good shot!" called the men.

"It was a good shot," said Robin.

Now he picked out an arrow himself. He stepped forward. He did not seem to aim. He sent the arrow flying. Straight at the target it went. It hit the stranger's arrow and split it apart. Robin's men cheered. The stranger's mouth hung open.

"I don't believe it," he said. He looked at Robin. Then he looked at the arrow again. He smiled and held out his hand. "You win," he said. "I'll be glad to be one of you. You're a better man than I am after all." The men laughed. Will Stutely stepped forward.

"If you become one of us," he said, "we've got to name you. Come, I'll be your godfather. What is your name?"

"John Little," said the stranger.

"Why," said Will, "I don't like that at all. We'll change it." He stooped down and filled his hat with water. He stood on his toes and poured the water over the stranger's head. "From now on you're Little John," he cried. Robin and his men laughed. The water ran down Little John's face and neck. At last he laughed too.

And that is how John Little became Little John, and Robin's right-hand man.

How Robin and His Men Saved Will Stutely

The Sheriff was worried. "I wish I had not told the King about Robin Hood," he said. "Now I will have to catch him. The King will soon ask about him. I've tried but I can't catch him. Well, I'll try again."

So he called all his men together. "Men," he said, "we are going to Sherwood Forest to get Robin Hood. Each one of you take four men with you. Go into Sherwood in bands of five. Each one take a horn along. When you see one of Robin's men, blow the horn. All the others will come running to help you. I want Robin Hood dead or alive. I will give one hundred silver coins to the one who gets him.

You get fifty silver coins for each of Robin's men you catch. Get your swords and bows ready."

So hundreds of men went into the forest. Day after day they looked for Robin and his men. But Robin's friends had told him they were coming. The Sheriff's men saw not one man in Lincoln green.

Robin's men had wanted to fight the Sheriff's men.

"Master," said Will Stutely, "let us fight them. We know the woods. We can pick them off one by one. Then we'll be safe."

"No, Will," said Robin Hood. "You know why I have to hide. Once I killed a man. If we fight them, we will kill many of them. I would rather not kill them if I can help it. We will keep out of their way. They never will find us."

So Robin's men hid. Every day they hoped Robin would change his mind and let them fight. Robin saw they wanted to do something. At last he said:

"Men, let's find out what they are doing. Who wants to find out?"

Every man there raised his hand. "Send me! Send me!" cried everyone. Robin laughed.

"We all can't go. Will Stutely, you know the woods best. Find out where they are and come back and tell us."

So Will got a churchman's robe and put it on over his Lincoln green. Off he went through the woods, his head down as if he were praying. No one could see the heavy sword strapped to his side.

Soon Will came to the end of the forest. Here he began to meet the Sheriff's men. But he just put his head down and kept going. At last he came to an inn. A crowd of the Sheriff's men was there, resting and drinking. Will sat down on a bench.

As he sat there a cat came out and began to rub against his leg. Will pushed the cat away, but it was too late. One of the Sheriff's men saw a green leg under the black robe. He looked at Will carefully.

"Churchmen don't wear Lincoln green under their robes," he said to himself.

"That is one of Robin Hood's men. Here is where I make myself fifty silver coins." He got up and walked over to Will. "Holy man," he said, "won't you have a pot of beer? It's hot today. Have a cool drink on me."

Will just shook his head.

"Where are you going, holy man?" he asked.

"To Nottingham," said Will.

"And why do you wear Lincoln green under your robe?" he shouted suddenly. "You're no churchman! You're one of Robin Hood's men!" He jumped forward, pulling out his sword.

But Will was a fast man with a sword, too. He jumped up and pulled out his own sword. The Sheriff's man swung a mighty blow. Will hit it aside. He stepped close and smashed his sword on the other's head. The man's eyes rolled and he fell forward. As he fell he grabbed at Will. He caught hold of the robe. Will tried to pull loose, but the man held on. The others jumped in to help. Will got another one, but there were too many. They piled on him and tied him up. In a few minutes they were riding to Nottingham.

Back in Sherwood Forest Robin Hood waited for news from Will. When he did not come, Robin sent some men after him. At last one man came running back.

"They have caught Will!" he cried. Robin's men gathered around him. "He is hurt. They have taken him to Nottingham. The people say he will be hanged tomorrow."

"He shall not be hanged tomorrow," said Robin. "If he is, many a man will die first. What do you say, men? Does Will Stutely hang tomorrow?"

"No! No!" cried the men.

Early the next morning Robin's men dressed in old clothes. By twos and threes they set out for Nottingham. They met in the woods just outside the city.

"Get into Nottingham," said Robin. "Mix with the people. Stay close together. When the soldiers come out with Will, move close. When they get outside the city walls, get next to the soldiers. Do nothing till I give the signal. Then we'll take him away. Stick together until we get into the forest again. Ready?"

"Ready!"

In Nottingham the streets were full. Everybody knew Will Stutely was to be hanged that day. Soon the castle gates opened and the Sheriff's men came riding out. Then came the Sheriff, riding proudly in shining armor. Behind him came a little wagon. In it sat Will Stutely. A rope was around his neck and blood was on his face.

He looked at the crowd. Not a friendly face was near him yet.

"Looking for your friends?" laughed the Sheriff. "You'll hang like a dog. When I lay hands on your master, I'll hang him, too. I'll hang every last man in Sherwood Forest."

"Ha!" laughed Will. "You coward! Give me a sword and I'll fight all of you right now! You catch Robin Hood! Don't make me laugh. I dare you to give me a sword."

"No," said the Sheriff. "You're a robber. You will die like an outlaw — you'll hang! You're afraid! You're afraid to die."

"We'll see who is afraid when Robin Hood hears of this," said Will. The Sheriff rode on and said no more. Will bowed his head.

When they came to the city walls he looked around him. His heart jumped. Here and there he saw faces he knew. Robin's men were moving in closer to the wagon. He saw Robin himself and Little John close to the Sheriff. Now the outlaws began to push the Sheriff's men aside.

"Get back there!" shouted the Sheriff. "What do you mean by pushing in there? Get back, I say."

One of the soldiers tried to push Little John away.

"Get back, you big ox," he cried.

"Get back yourself," said Little John. He hit the man on the head with his great fist. The guard dropped quietly from his horse. Little John jumped lightly into the wagon. With one swing he cut the ropes.

"Hello, Will," he said. "You didn't think we had forgotten you, did you? If you die, we die with you. Come on, jump."

"Stop them! Stop them!" cried the Sheriff. "I know him! That's Little John, the outlaw! Get him, men!" He rode at Little John and swung his sword. But Little John ducked under the Sheriff's horse and came up on the other side. He pulled the sword out of the Sheriff's hand.

"Dear Sheriff," he said, "you must lend us your sword. Here, Will, the Sheriff wants you to have his sword." The Sheriff backed his horse away quickly.

Now swords flashed all around the guards. The arrows began to fly.

"Run!" cried the Sheriff. "They'll kill us!" He turned and rode for the city. His men followed as fast as they could. Robin and his men moved toward the forest.

"Come back, Sheriff," called Will Stutely. "Aren't you going to hang us?" But the Sheriff only rode faster. It was a long time before the Sheriff rode outside of Nottingham again.

LITTLE JOHN MEETS HIS MATCH

Robin and his men were lying under the trees in Sherwood Forest. Suddenly Robin jumped up.

"Say, men," he cried, "I almost forgot. We are out of Lincoln green cloth. We won't have anything to wear soon. Come on, Little John. Move your lazy bones. You are getting fat. Get over to town. Buy us enough green cloth for new suits."

Little John grunted. "Maybe I am getting fat. I'll bet I could still hold my place on a bridge, though. I seem to remember knocking a fellow into the water. He wasn't very fat, either."

The outlaws laughed and looked at

Robin. They all knew Little John had knocked Robin off the bridge. Robin laughed harder than anybody.

"Right you are, Little John," he said. "You're a better man with the cudgel than I. But can you beat me with a bow and arrow yet?"

Little John laughed. "No, not yet. You've got me there."

"Wait," said Robin, "I'll get the money." He jumped up. Soon he came back with a bag of money. Little John put it in his shirt, picked up his cudgel, and started out.

Soon he came to the inn where Will Stutely had been caught. He heard the men laughing inside. He thought of the cool drinks. He looked at the dusty road. He scratched his head. Then he looked at the clear blue sky. But not a cloud was there.

"It looks like rain," said Little John to himself. "I'd better stop here a little while. Robin wouldn't want me to get wet." So he went in.

The inn was full of men drinking and

singing. Little John was soon having a good time. He slept at the inn that night. In the morning he started out again.

In the town nearby lived a famous leather worker named Arthur Bland. He was a great strong man. He had been a wrestling champion for five years. He had lost at last, but no one had ever beaten him with the cudgel. Arthur liked to hunt, too. He would slip out to the forest when the deer hunting was good. The king's woodsmen kept a close eye on Arthur.

Arthur had been selling cow hides in Nottingham. As he came past Sherwood Forest on his way home, he looked into the dark forest.

"Now I wonder," he said, "if I could see a deer today."

He stepped lightly into the forest. Quietly he pushed the bushes aside. He looked left and right.

Just then Little John came by. He saw Arthur slip into the woods.

"Now what is he up to?" asked Little John. "I'll just follow him and see."

So Arthur looked for deer and Little John watched Arthur. Then Little John stepped on a stick. It broke. Arthur jumped and turned around. Little John stepped into the open.

"Now, my man," he said, "what are you doing? You look like a bad one to me. Hunting deer, are you?"

But Arthur Bland was not afraid at all.

"You're a liar," he said. "And you don't look very good to me yourself."

"Ha!" cried Little John. "Talk back, will you? I think I'll crack you on your thick head."

"Let's see you do it."

"All right," cried Little John. "Get your cudgel ready. You're going to get a good beating."

Each man grabbed his cudgel and walked toward the other.

One of the outlaws had seen Little John at the inn. When Robin heard about it, he was angry.

"I'll tell him something when I catch him," he said. "Loafing at the inn again!"

Robin set out after him. As he walked through the woods he heard loud voices. He stopped and listened.

"That sounds like Little John," he said. "He must be in trouble." He forgot he was angry. Quietly he moved forward. Pushing the bushes aside he saw Little John and Arthur Bland. "Ah," smiled Robin, "a fight! I'd like to see that fellow give Little John a beating. He might learn to stay away from that inn. But I don't think anybody can beat him. Well, I'll watch." He lay down behind some thick bushes.

Little John and Arthur Bland were walking around each other slowly. Both were waiting for a good chance. Suddenly Little John struck. Whack! Arthur turned the blow aside. He hit back like a flash. The fight was on!

Back and forth they went, tearing up the ground. They began to breathe hard. Little John was too fat now for a long fight.

Robin could hardly keep from laughing aloud. "He is too fat to last long," he said to himself. "This may teach him a lesson. He can beat that fellow, but not today. That stranger is a good fighter."

Then Little John saw his chance. He swung his cudgel. But Arthur was lucky. He had on a thick cowhide cap. Little John hit him a hard blow on the head. Arthur almost went down. Had Little John not been tired, he could have won the fight then.

But Arthur stayed on his feet. He came back swinging fast and hard. Before Little John could raise his arms, Arthur hit him. Whack! Little John hit the ground. His cudgel went flying. Now Arthur had him. He began to beat Little John's ribs.

"Stop!" cried Little John. "Will you hit a man when he's down?"

"Will I?" said Arthur. "Watch me. There, take that!" Again he hit him.

"Ouch! Help! You crazy fool! I give up."

"You had enough?" asked Arthur. Again he raised his arms.

"Yes!" shouted Little John.

"Then get up and get out of here. You're lucky I don't hit you again."

"All right, all right." Little John felt his sore ribs. He got slowly to his feet.

Robin could keep still no longer. He laughed until the tears rolled down his cheeks. He came out of the bushes.

"I wouldn't have believed it," he said. "Little John, I never had so much fun. How do your ribs feel? Wait till the men hear about this."

But Little John would say nothing. He just looked sour.

"And who are you, my fine fellow?" said Robin to Arthur.

"My name is Arthur Bland," he said. "Who are you?"

"Arthur Bland! Ah, we've heard of you, Arthur. That fellow lying there is the famous Little John. I am Robin Hood."

"What?" cried Arthur. "You are the great Robin Hood? And this is the famous Little John? If I had known that, I would never have fought you. Come, let me help you up."

"Oh, I can get up," said Little John. "But don't forget that cowhide cap saved you."

Robin laughed again. Then he turned to Arthur. "Arthur Bland, you're a good fighter. How would you like to become one of us?"

"Become one of your men?" cried Arthur. "Well, I should say I would. I'd like nothing better."

"Good," said Robin. "Now, Little John, Arthur and I will go with you. We still need that green cloth. You may come to another inn, you know. Or somebody else may beat your fat ribs for you."

So, arm in arm, off went the three through Sherwood Forest.

Robin Hood
MEETS WILL SCARLET

Robin, Arthur, and Little John went on to buy the cloth they needed. Suddenly Robin stopped.

"Say," he said, "why did you stop at the inn? Why didn't you go on as I told you?"

"Why," said Little John, "I was afraid it was going to rain."

"What?" cried Robin. "Rain? Why, you big ox, we haven't seen a cloud for three days!"

"Well," said Little John, "it could have rained."

"Ha! Ha! Ha!" laughed Robin. "How can anybody stay angry with you? I give up. But you'll hear more of this. Wait till

I tell the men. Wait till they hear how Arthur beat your ribs sore."

So on they went, arm in arm, laughing. Soon they came to a brook. The day was hot, so they stopped to drink. Then they sat down to rest. Little John and Arthur were almost asleep when Robin spoke.

"Look," he said. "Isn't that a pretty boy coming down the road?"

Arthur and Little John turned to look. A young man was walking toward them. His coat and long stockings were a beautiful red silk. His cap, too, was scarlet, with a big red feather. His hair was bright yellow and hung to his shoulders. A fine sword hung at his side. He carried a rose in his hand. He raised the rose to his nose and smelled it.

"Did you ever see anything like that before?" asked Robin Hood. "He makes me sick."

"Well," said Arthur Bland, "I don't like his clothes, either. But take a good look. Look at those shoulders. Look at his arms. He is stronger than you think."

"You're right, Arthur," said Little John. "Looks to me as if he's trying to fool people."

"Bah!" cried Robin. "Watch him smell that rose. A man smelling a rose! I wonder who he is."

"Some rich man's son, I guess," said Little John. "I'll bet he's got some money."

"Well," said Robin, "I think we should have it. The poor people need more help. Fellows like this never work and still are rich. Now you think he's a pretty good man, don't you? Well, I'll show you. You two hide here. I'll go out and stop him. Watch me give him a good beating, Little John. Maybe you won't let yourself get so fat and lazy when you see me beat him."

Robin got up and stood in the road. The stranger kept walking slowly toward him. Robin stood in his way.

"Stop," called Robin. "Stand still."

The stranger smelled his rose again. Then he looked at Robin with a soft smile. He spoke softly and gently.

"And why, dear fellow, should I stop? Do you want to speak to me? I'll be glad to listen."

"Well," said Robin, "that's very good of you. I'll tell you what I want. I would like to get a little money together to help the poor. Haven't you got a fat money bag on you?"

The stranger was smelling his rose again. "No," he said. "I'm sorry. I have no money for you, dear fellow. I'll have to be going. Anything else?"

"Come on, come on," said Robin. "Let's have the money."

"Oh, no, I couldn't think of it. Will you please step aside, dear fellow?"

"You don't go until you give me your money," said Robin. He raised his cudgel.

"Now, isn't that too bad!" said the stranger sadly. "I guess I'll have to kill you, dear fellow. I just hate to do this." He pulled his sword loose.

"Put that thing away," said Robin. "I could break that sword with this oak cudgel. You are asking for a beating. Go get yourself a cudgel over there. There are some oak trees. Cut off a cudgel and take your beating."

The stranger looked at Robin. Then he looked at Robin's strong oak cudgel.

"Dear fellow," he said, "I think you're right. Wait just a minute. I'll get myself a cudgel."

He walked over to the oak trees. He stopped before a straight young tree. He reached down and calmly pulled it out of the ground. Then he walked back cutting the roots and little branches away.

Little John and Arthur looked at each other. Little John gave a soft whistle.

"Did you see that, Arthur?" he asked.

"Pulled up a tree!" said Arthur.

"I can't believe my eyes," said Little John. "I wouldn't like to fight him! Robin will have his hands full."

Robin and the stranger now faced each other. Soon the cudgels were flying. Never had Robin fought so well. Robin was the faster and more clever with his cudgel. But never had he fought so strong a man.

When the stranger hit Robin's cudgel, he nearly knocked it from his hands. Robin's hands were soon sore. And he had to fight carefully. One blow would have laid him flat, and he knew it. The stranger was stronger even than Little John. And Little John could kill a horse with his cudgel.

"Crack!" Robin hit like lightning and rapped the stranger's arm. He did not seem to feel it. Crack! Robin got him again, this time in the ribs. Then, once more he got him. But the stranger just grunted. He swung his cudgel hard. Robin turned the blow. But the stranger hit Robin's cudgel so hard that Robin's hands and arms went down. The stranger hit again. Again Robin blocked the blow. This time his cudgel fell from his hands. The stranger caught him across the chest now. Down went Robin in the dust.

"Stop!" shouted Little John. He jumped to Robin's side. Arthur Bland followed.

"Well!" said the stranger calmly. "Two more! If you're as good as he is, I'm through. But, come on. I'll do my best."

"No," cried Robin. "We fight no more. Little John, this is our unlucky day. We both got ourselves a good beating. I feel as if a horse had kicked me."

Little John remembered how Robin had laughed at him. He began to smile.

"Poor master," he said, "how your ribs must hurt! And how sorry our friends will be! Just wait until I tell them how you got beat. Here, let me help you up."

Now it was Robin's turn to look sour. "I can get up myself," he said. He got up and turned to the stranger. "Who are you? What is your name?"

"Gamewell," said the stranger.

"Gamewell?" said Robin. "Why, I know — where are you from?"

"From Locksley. I'm running away. I'm looking for the famous outlaw, Robin Hood. He's my cousin. Can you tell me where to find him?"

"Will Gamewell!" cried Robin. "Don't you know me, Will? I should have known you! But it's been years since I saw you."

"You are Robin Hood!" cried the other.

"I can see it now. You are Robin Hood himself — my cousin, Robert Fitzooth."

"Cousin Will, you're the strongest man I ever saw. But I remember you always were a strong boy. Tell me, how is your father? Why are you running away?"

"It was like this. Father had a man taking care of things after you left. I never liked him. But father said he needed him. The fellow was a friend of the Sheriff. He said what he wished to father. One day I heard him. Well, I hit him on the jaw. And what do you think? He died! They said I had broken his neck. I knew the Sheriff would be after me, so here I am. I don't feel like hanging — yet."

"Well, you didn't seem to be in a hurry," said Robin. "You were smelling a rose! But we're glad you're here, Will. We're glad you want to be one of us. We'll have to change your name. We all get a new name in Sherwood Forest."

"He ought to be Will Scarlet," cried Arthur. "His clothes are scarlet."

"Will Scarlet you shall be," said Robin.

"Will Scarlet, I'm glad to have you, too," said Little John. "Our men will hear another good story now." Little John looked at Robin. "They'll laugh many a day to hear about our Robin Hood's beating."

"Little John," said Robin smiling, "shut up. You've got me as I had you. I won't tell the men about you and Arthur."

"You don't think I'm getting too fat, do you?"

"No, Little John, you're not too fat."

"You did think it would rain last night, didn't you?"

"Why, yes, it did look like rain."

"It was wise for me to stay at the inn, wasn't it?"

"Yes, Little John, it was."

"Ah!" smiled Little John. "Then I didn't see you get a beating today."

All four broke out laughing. They picked up their cudgels and started back into the forest.

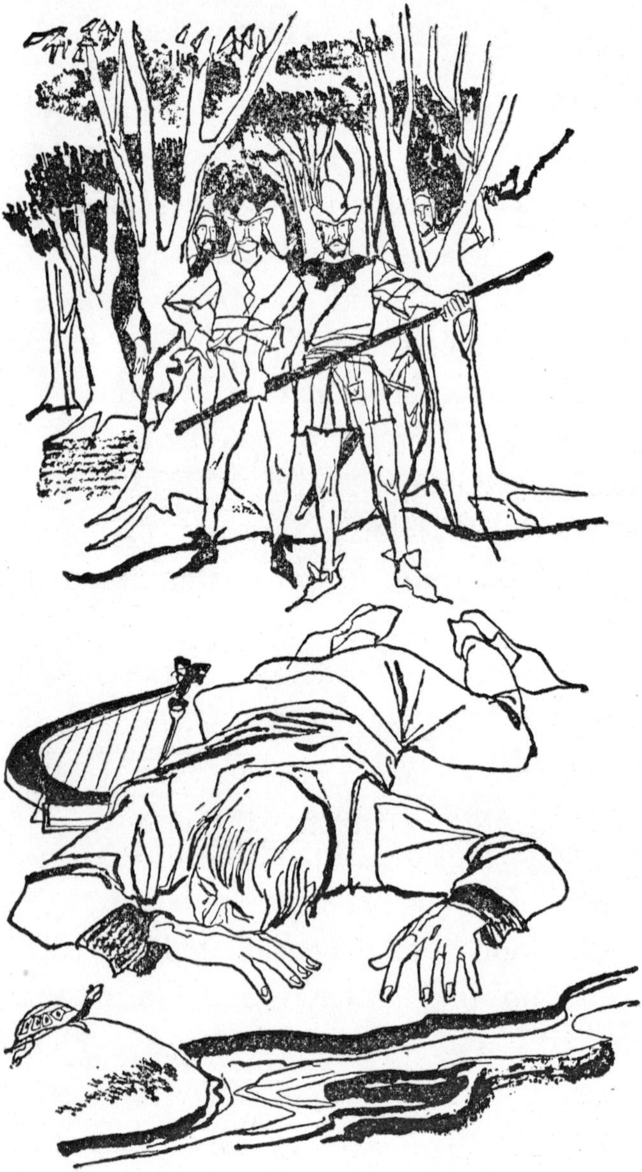

Allan-a-Dale
COMES TO SHERWOOD FOREST

When rich people came through Sherwood Forest, Robin Hood and his men often robbed them. They took the money and gave it to the poor. They liked to catch the rich men and take them deep into the forest. There Robin's men would cook a fine dinner. Robin and his men would be very kind to their prisoners. They waited on them and gave them the best food. During the dinner there would be music — playing and singing. After dinner there would be sports. The men would wrestle or box or have shooting matches. When it was all over, the rich prisoner would have to give up his gold and silver.

Then Robin's men would show him the way out of the forest.

A few days after Will Scarlet came to Sherwood, Robin and his men were taking it easy.

"Men," said Robin, "we have had nobody to eat with us for a long time. The gold is running low. Will Stutely, you take a few men and bring us a good fat rich man to have dinner with us."

So Will Stutely chose Will Scarlet, Arthur Bland, and a few others to go along. They went down to a broad road over which many people came. Here they hid behind the trees to wait.

The hours went by. Many came over the road, but none whom Will wanted. First came a few girls, then a poor farmer or two. A boy came by with his sheep, and then a few old women. Not one rich man came by. At last the sun began to go down. Will Stutely got up.

"Such bad luck!" he said. "We have waited all day for nothing. Come, men, let's go home."

The men got up and followed Will. They had gone a few steps when Will stopped.

"I hear something," he said. "Be quiet."

At last they could hear a voice crying.

"Ha!" cried Will Scarlet. "Somebody is in trouble. Let's find him and help him."

They slipped softly through the trees. Soon they came to a pool of water. On the bank lay a boy, crying.

"Hello!" cried Will Stutely. "Who are you, boy? Why are you crying like a girl!"

The boy jumped up, took his bow, and put an arrow to it.

"I know him," said one of the men. "He is the boy who goes from place to place playing and singing."

"Come, boy," cried Will Stutely. "I hate to see a boy crying. Put your bow away. We are not going to hurt you."

Will Scarlet walked over and put his arm on the boy's shoulder. "Come," he said kindly. "Are you in trouble? These men will not hurt you. Come with us. We know someone who will help you."

The boy picked up his harp and followed them. Through the forest they went to their camp. Soon they could see the fires and smell the meat cooking. Will and his little band marched to the tree where Robin and Little John were sitting.

"Good evening, friend," said Robin. "Have you come to eat with me today?"

"I don't know," said the boy. "It all seems like a dream —"

"Well," laughed Robin, "we'll soon wake you up."

The boy looked around him. Then he turned back to Robin.

"I think I know where I am now," he said. "Are you not the great Robin Hood?"

"Right you are," said Robin. "I guess you know everybody who eats with us pays his way. I hope you have a fat purse of gold with you?"

"I have no gold," said the stranger sadly.

"What?" said Robin, looking at Will Stutely. "Why do you bring him here, Will?"

"The boy is in trouble, master," said Will Scarlet.

Robin laid his hand on the boy's shoulder.

"Come, boy, cheer up," he said. "What is your name?"

"Allan-a-Dale, master."

"Why," said Robin, "you are the singer we hear about. Everybody says you have a beautiful voice. Now tell us your trouble."

Allan told how he had gone from castle to castle to sing and play. He had come to a farm house on the way. The farmer and his beautiful daughter Ellen had listened. Allan could not forget the girl. He had gone back to see Ellen when he could. At last he told her he loved her. Ellen said that she loved him, too.

But then the father had found out he was seeing her. He did not want her to marry a poor singer, so he would not let them meet.

"And then," said Allan, "I got news that my Ellen is to be married. Married to a rich old man called Sir Stephen! Her father is making her marry him for his money. She does not love him."

"Why," cried Little John, "an old man marrying a young girl! He ought to be beaten, and I can do it!"

"But, Allan," said Will Scarlet, "why does she do it? I don't like it."

"She can't help herself," cried Allan. "She may do what her father tells her, but her heart will break. She will die! I know she will die!"

Robin had been thinking.

"I have a plan, Allan. Suppose you and Ellen were in church and a priest was there. Would she marry you even if her father said no?"

"Yes, she would!" cried Allan.

"If her father is the man I think he is, I will get him to say yes. But wait — we need a priest. Where can we get one? They are not very friendly with me."

"I know one," said Will Scarlet. "If you could get on his good side, he would do it. His name is Friar Tuck. He is not afraid of anybody. I know where he lives."

"All right, Allan," cried Robin. "In two days Ellen will be your wife. I will go see this holy man tomorrow. If he does not want to help us, I'll beat a little help into him."

Will Scarlet laughed. "Don't be too sure of that, good cousin," he said. "But I think he will help if there is a chance for some good food and drink."

Now the men called that dinner was ready. Everybody sat down to eat. When they had finished, Robin turned to Allan-a-Dale.

"Now, Allan," he said, "sing for us."

Allan picked up his harp and sang for them. Never had the men heard so sweet a voice. He sang song after song.

"Allan," said Robin at last, "you just have to stay with us. You must live in the green forest with us."

"I will stay with you always, master," said Allan.

And that is how Allan-a-Dale became one of Robin Hood's band in Sherwood Forest.

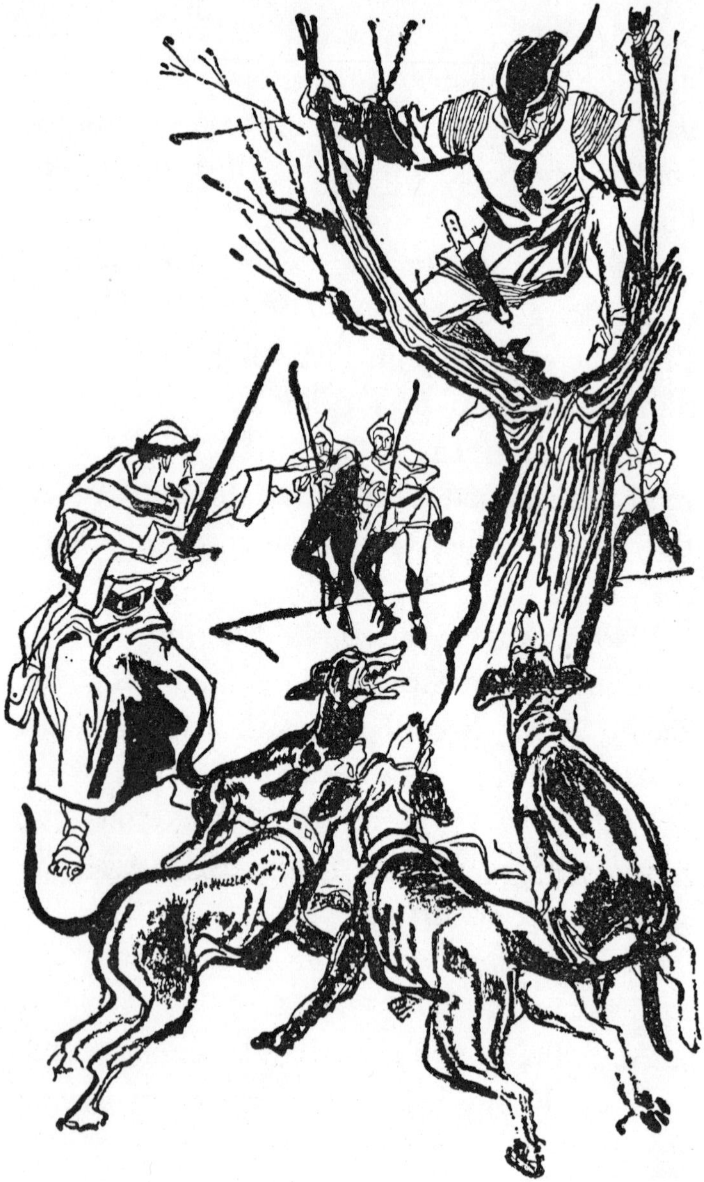

ROBIN HOOD
FINDS FRIAR TUCK

Robin got up early next morning.

"Now I am going to see this holy man, this Friar Tuck. I will take four of you. Little John, Will Scarlet, Arthur Bland, and David of Doncaster, get ready. Will Stutely will be chief while I am gone."

Then Robin put on a coat of steel. Over this he put on his Lincoln green coat. On his head he put a steel cap. He covered it with one of soft white leather. Next he strapped his big sword to his side.

And so the five started out. Will Scarlet led the way, for he knew where to go.

A little after noon they came to a wide stream. Will went on along the stream.

"Now, cousin," he said at last, "just around that bend is a place to cross. On the other side lives Friar Tuck. Come, I will show you."

"No," said Robin. "Stay here. I did not want to get wet, but I guess I must. You men all stay here. I will go alone. If I need you, I will blow my horn."

When Robin got around the bend, he stopped to listen. He was sure he had heard voices. Then he heard them again. A voice spoke and another answered. The voices were almost alike. Robin could hear that they came from the bushes on the bank.

"That's strange!" said Robin. "Those voices are alike."

He pushed the bushes aside. Sitting against a tree was a big strong fellow. Nobody else was near. His head was round as a bull's. Black hair grew around his head, but the top was smooth as an egg. He wore a long black robe. The string of beads showed he was a friar. His cheeks were red as apples. He had a short thick neck. The shoulders were broad as Little John's. Under his black eyebrows his little gray eyes danced. A steel cap lay beside him. His legs were stretched wide apart. Between his knees he held a big bowl of meat and onions. He held a big piece of bread in one hand. First he took a bite of bread. Then he stuck his hand into the meat. When his mouth was full, he took a long drink from a beer bottle.

"Well!" said Robin. "This holy man must have been talking to himself."

Robin sat down to watch him.

At last the friar was done. He picked up his beer bottle and began talking to himself again.

"Dear fellow," he said, "you are the best fellow in the world. I do like you so much. Will you not have a drink?"

Now he handed the bottle over to his left hand. He changed his voice a little.

"Why, yes," he said. "I'll be glad to have a drink."

Here he put the bottle to his lips and took a long drink.

"And now, dear fellow," he said, "it is your turn."

He held the bottle in the other hand and drank again. All this time Robin could hardly keep from laughing. Then the friar put his bottle down.

"And now, sweet fellow," he said, "let us have a song."

Now he began to sing a song. First he sang in one voice, then in another, as if two men were singing. Robin could keep still no longer. He sang the last few lines with him and gave a loud laugh.

The friar jumped to his feet. He picked up his steel cap and put it on.

"What spy have we here?" he cried. "Come out, coward! I'll cut you up like a piece of meat."

The friar reached under his long robe and pulled out a sword.

"No, friend," laughed Robin. "Put your sword away. We have nothing to fight about."

Robin jumped down to where the other stood.

"I tell you, friend, I could use a drink. Is there anything left in that bottle?"

"You might wait until I ask you," said the friar. "But I am a man of the church and do good to all men. Here, take a drink."

Robin took the bottle and drank what was left. The friar looked at the empty bottle sadly.

"My good man," said Robin, "do you know Friar Tuck?"

"Yes, I know him."

"I would like to cross the stream and go see him."

"Well, why don't you do it?"

"Good father," said Robin, "you can see I have on good clothes. I don't want to get them wet. You have such broad shoulders. You could easily carry me over."

"Why, you — you — what shall I call you?" cried the friar. "I, a holy friar, should carry you?" He stopped. The anger went out of his face. His little eyes danced. "But holy men do help others," he said. "Why not? I will do it."

He stepped down to the water, laughing to himself. He pulled up his robe and put his sword under his arm.

"You may get your sword wet," said the friar. "Let me carry it for you."

Robin handed him his sword. Now the friar bent over and Robin got on. The friar walked on into the water. Soon he put him down on the other side.

"Thanks, father," he said. "You are a good and holy man. Now give me my sword. I'll be on my way. I am in a hurry."

The friar had a smile on his face. He closed one eye.

"Yes," he said, "I know you are in a hurry. But have you thought of me? I want to get to the other side. If I get wet again I might get sick. I know you will carry me back. Don't forget I have two swords. You have none. Let's go."

Robin Hood bit his lip.

"I might have known you are not the man you seemed to be," he said.

"Let's not talk like that," said the friar. "You may feel an inch or two of steel."

"All right," said Robin. "Give me my sword. I give you my word I will not use it."

"Here," said the friar, "take it. I'm not afraid of you. Get ready, I want to go."

So Robin took his sword and bent his back. The friar jumped on.

Now the friar was a heavier load than Robin had been. Robin did not know the stream. He kept falling over the stones. Now and then he stepped into a deep hole. The sweat ran down his face. The friar dug his heels into Robin's side and called him names.

Robin did not say a word. Softly he felt for the friar's sword belt. Slowly he worked the sword loose. When Robin stepped on land, he pulled the sword free.

"Now," said Robin, "I have you. Who has two swords now? Now you carry me back or I'll poke you full of holes."

"All right," said the friar. "You have me. Give me my sword. I promise to carry you."

So Robin gave him his sword again.

The friar put it into his belt. This time he pulled it tight. He took Robin up and stepped into the water. Robin sat on his back laughing.

At last they reached the middle of the stream. The friar shook his big shoulders and bent over. Robin went flying over his head. He landed with a splash.

"There," said the friar. "Let that cool you off."

Robin got up. He spit water out of his mouth. He wiped it from his eyes. The friar was on the bank laughing. Robin was angry as he could be.

"Wait, you!" he cried. "I'm coming after you."

He ran up to the bank.

"Don't hurry," said the friar. "I will not run away. I'll give you the beating of your life if you want to fight."

Robin rolled up his sleeves. The friar pulled back his robe. His arm was thick as a small tree trunk. Robin saw that the friar, too, wore a steel coat.

"Ready?" called Robin.

"Ready!" the friar's voice rang out clear.

Then began a mighty battle. Up and down the bank they fought. The swords struck together like thunder. First Robin drove the friar back. Then the friar stormed back at Robin.

They fought for an hour, stopping now and then to rest. They looked at each other. Each knew he had never fought a better man. At last Robin cried, "Stop!" They lowered their swords.

"I'm going to ask you a favor," said Robin. He wiped the sweat from his face.

"What do you want?" asked the friar.

"Only this — let me blow my horn three times."

"This is some kind of trick," said the friar. "But I still am not afraid of you. Go ahead. But you must let me blow three times on this little whistle."

"All right," said Robin. "Here we go." He raised his horn and blew three times.

The four men in Lincoln green came running down the road. Each had his bow and arrow ready.

"I thought so!" cried the friar. He blew his whistle three times before anyone could stop him. Sounds of running feet came from the bushes. In a minute four big hunting dogs came running to the friar.

"Get him!" cried the friar pointing at Robin.

Robin dropped his sword and jumped for a tree. He pulled his feet up just as the dogs got there. The friar pointed at Robin's men.

"Get them!" he cried.

All but Will Scarlet let fly with their arrows. But the dogs jumped to one side as the arrows were about to hit them. The dogs turned, got the arrows, and snapped them with their big teeth. Then they sprang after the men again.

It would have been a sad day for Robin's men had Will Scarlet not stepped forward.

"Down, boy!" he cried. "Down!"

The dogs came up to Will and licked his hands.

"Here!" cried the friar. "What are you

doing with my dogs? Oh, Will Gamewell, it is you! What are you doing here?"

"No, Friar," laughed Will. "I am now Will Scarlet. This is my cousin, Robin Hood. I live with him in Sherwood Forest."

Robin came down from his tree. The friar held out his hand.

"I have heard of you, master," he said. "No wonder you were such a fighter. I'm sorry. I did not know you."

"That's all right," said Robin. "But we had better go find the friar I was looking for. It is getting late."

"Why," laughed Will Scarlet, "Friar Tuck is the one I meant. This *is* Friar Tuck!"

"What? You are the one I wanted?"

"Why, yes. My name is Friar Tuck."

"Why didn't you tell me?"

"You didn't ask me."

"Well," laughed Robin, "come along. It is getting late. Come back to Sherwood with us, Friar Tuck. We need your help."

And so the men, with the dogs at their heels, made their way back to Sherwood.

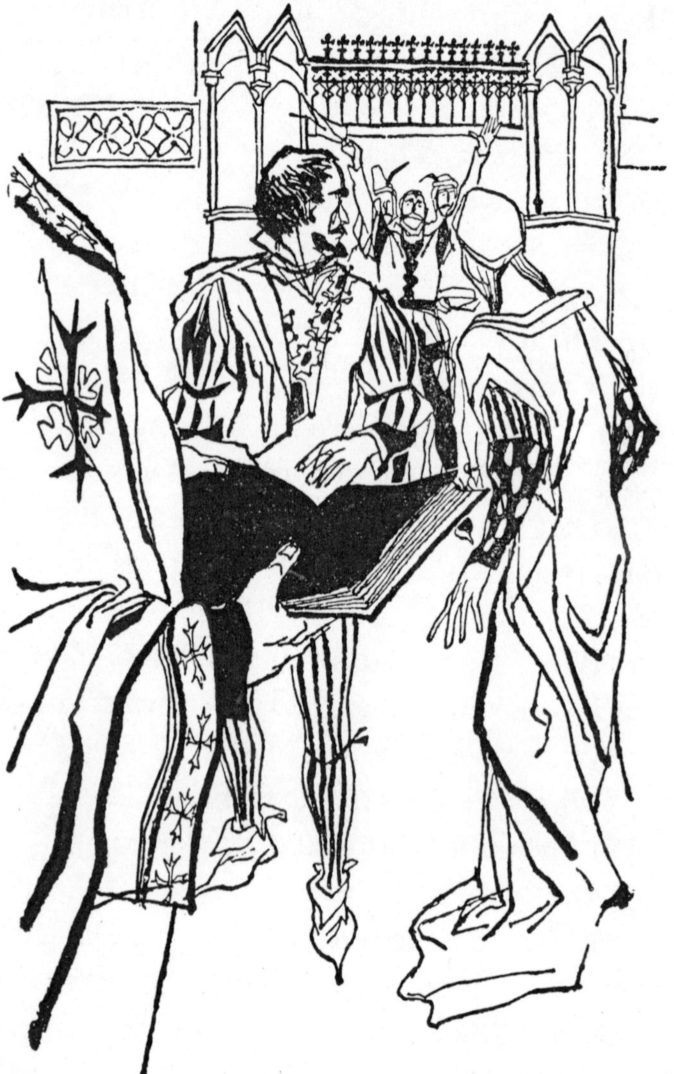

ROBIN HOOD
GOES TO A WEDDING

Now came the day when Ellen was to marry the rich Sir Stephen. Robin and his men got up early.

"It is time to go," said Robin. "I'll need about twenty men to go with me. I may need some help. Will Scarlet, you stay and be chief while I am gone."

Then Robin picked the men who were to go. As they got themselves ready, Robin stepped behind the bushes. When he came out he had on a bright-colored coat such as singers wore. Over his shoulder he carried a harp. He wore long green stockings and a tall red leather hat. He handed two bags to Little John.

"Gold?" asked Little John wonderingly.

"Gold," said Robin. "Come, men." He led the way followed by Allan-a-Dale, Friar Tuck, and the others.

They came to the end of the forest and started down a broad road. On they went until they came to a little country church. Here the fair Ellen was to marry Sir Stephen.

Beside the road ran a stone wall. Robin and his men jumped over and lay down on the other side.

"David," called Robin, "keep watch on the road. Let us know when somebody comes."

The men lay quietly for a while. Then David spoke.

"I see an old friar. He is coming over the hill. He carries a big bunch of keys. He is turning to the church door."

Robin shook Friar Tuck, who had fallen asleep.

"Come, holy man," he said. "Go over and talk to the friar. See that you get inside. Little John, Will, and I will follow."

So Friar Tuck got over the wall and went up to the friar. The old man was trying to unlock the door.

"Hello, brother, let me help you," said Friar Tuck. He took the keys and opened the door.

"Who are you, brother?" asked the old man.

"I am Friar Tuck. I want to see this wedding."

"Glad to have you, brother," said the old man.

He led the way inside. Friar Tuck followed. Now came Robin, Will, and Little John. Robin sat down outside. Will and Little John slipped inside the church.

Soon Robin saw some men come riding slowly down the road.

"Aha!" said Robin. "My old enemy, the Bishop."

The Bishop wore rich silk clothes. Around his neck hung a gold chain. His cap and shoes were black velvet. Beside him rode another churchman. The others were the Bishop's men.

"He dresses too well for a holy man," said Robin. "The money came from poor people. I'll have to get a little back for them."

Now the Bishop and his men got to the church and saw Robin.

"Well, my good fellow," said the Bishop, "what are you doing here?"

"I am a singer and harp player," said Robin. "I can play better than anyone. I can make people dance even if they do not want to. If I can play at this wedding, I can make the girl love the man she marries."

"Can you?" said the Bishop. "If you can cause this girl to love Sir Stephen, I'll give you what you ask. Let me hear you."

"No," said Robin. "I will not play until the wedding."

"You are not wise to speak so to me," said the Bishop. "But I see Sir Stephen and his lady coming. I will speak to you later."

A tall thin man in black silk came riding down the road. Robin saw his white hair and guessed it was Sir Stephen. Beside him rode Ellen's father. Next came the fair Ellen, followed by a few men in armor.

When they got to the church Sir Stephen helped Ellen down. When Robin saw her he knew why Allan loved her.

"She is the prettiest girl I have ever seen," said he. "I can see why this rich Sir Stephen wants to marry her."

But Ellen hung her head. Sadly she went into the church with Sir Stephen.

"Well," said the Bishop to Robin, "why don't you play?"

"I'll play when I'm ready," said Robin.

"I'll have you whipped if you do not take care," said the Bishop.

He went into the church and put on his robe. Ellen and Sir Stephen stood before him. Poor Ellen looked around like a hunted deer. Robin walked in and stood between her and Sir Stephen.

"Let me have a look at this girl," he said loudly. "She looks sad. Why, you, sir, are so old and she is so young! You want to marry her? She does not love you!"

Before anybody could move, Robin pulled out his horn. Three times he blew. Before he finished, Will Stutely and Little John were beside him, swords drawn. A great voice called from the back of the church. "Here I am when you want me, master!" cried Friar Tuck.

Now there was noise. Ellen's father stepped up to drag his girl away. Little John stepped in his way. He put his big hand in his face and pushed.

"Stand back, old man," he said.

"Down with them," cried Sir Stephen. His men pulled out their swords and started after Robin. But then came a rush of feet. Eighteen men in Lincoln green came running in, led by Allan-a-Dale.

"You are making this trouble, Allan-a-Dale," cried Ellen's father.

"No," said Robin Hood. "I am, and I don't care who knows it. My name is Robin Hood."

"Heaven help us," said the Bishop.

"I will not hurt you," said Robin. "But Ellen is going to marry Allan-a-Dale."

"I am her father! She shall marry Sir Stephen."

"No," said Sir Stephen, "you can have her. I will never marry her now. I did not know she loved this boy. Good-bye."

He walked out, his men following.

"I'll be going too," said the Bishop.

Robin reached out and held him.

"Wait," said Robin. "I want a word with you." He turned to Ellen's father.

"Give me the gold, Little John," he said. "Now, farmer, listen. Tell your girl to marry Allan-a-Dale and you get the gold. If you don't, she will marry him anyway and you get nothing. Choose."

"If she wants to, let her do it."

"Wait," said one of the Bishop's men. "There is no priest here to marry them."

"What?" roared a voice. "No priest? I am a holy man, I'll have you know. I'll be down there to change your mind."

Friar Tuck hurried to the front of the church. In a few minutes Ellen and Allan were married.

Then Robin turned to the Bishop.

"Lord Bishop," he said, "I know you want this girl to be happy. I think you have a wedding present for her, don't you?"

Here Robin lifted the gold chain from the Bishop's neck and put it around Ellen's.

The Bishop's face grew red and angry. He opened his mouth to say something. But when he looked at Robin he changed his mind.

"Thank you," said Robin. "That was a fine present. You look much better without it. Now if you ever get near Sherwood Forest, I'll give you a good dinner."

"Good heavens, no!" cried the Bishop. He had heard about Robin's dinners.

Now Robin got his men together. With Allan and his wife they turned back to Sherwood Forest. On the way Friar Tuck pulled Robin's sleeve.

"Don't you think you need a good holy man to stay with you always?" he asked.

Robin laughed. "You are welcome," he said. So Friar Tuck became one of Robin Hood's band.

ROBIN HOOD
HELPS A SAD KNIGHT

Robin Hood woke up early one fine morning. He stretched his arms and looked at Little John.

"This is a fine day, Little John. We should not waste it. You take some men and go one way. I will go the other way. Let's see if we cannot bring home a rich man to eat with us."

"Good!" cried Little John. "Let's go. I tell you I'll bring somebody home or I won't come home myself!" They each took some men and set out.

Robin and his men went on through fields and towns. When noon came they still had not found anyone. They had come

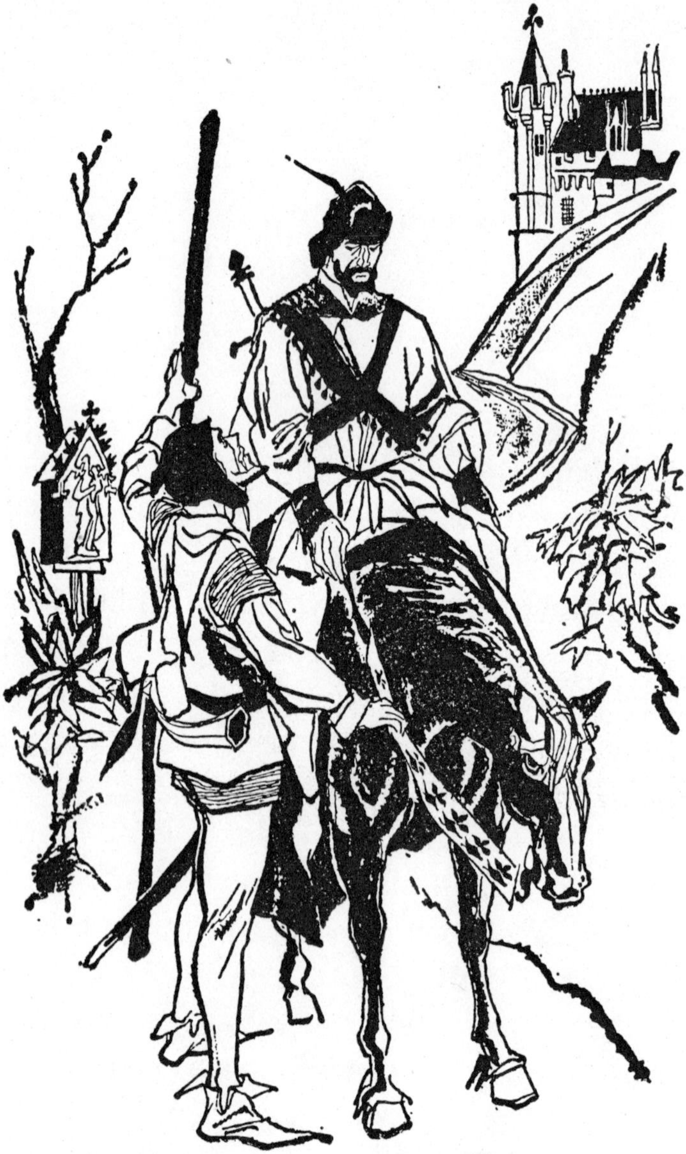

now to the crossing of two roads. Nearby were some tall bushes. Robin and his men sat behind them to eat their lunch. They could watch the road easily.

They had their lunch but stayed a while longer to watch. At last a man came riding slowly down the road. He looked like a good knight, but he hung his head and seemed very sad. His clothes were plain. He wore no gold chain or gold spurs as knights did in those days.

"There is a sorry-looking fellow," said Robin. "I'll go out and talk to him. He may have a fat bag of gold. Stay here until I find out."

Robin crossed the road and waited. When the knight came up to him, Robin stopped the horse.

"Stop, Sir Knight," he said. "I want to talk to you."

"Who are you?" said the knight. "Why do you stop me?"

"Who am I? That is hard to answer. Some people say I am a kind man. Some say I am a robber. I am Robin Hood."

The knight smiled. "I hear much good about you. What do you want from me?"

"Why, I would like you to come to Sherwood Forest to eat with us."

"You are very kind," said the knight. "But I think not. I do not feel very much like going."

"That would be all right," said Robin, "but we take a little gold from those who come."

"I see what you mean," said the knight. "I am not the right man. I have no money with me."

"No?" said Robin. "Some knights do not always tell the truth. You won't mind if I find out for myself?"

Now Robin whistled. The men in green came jumping through the bushes.

"These are my men," said Robin. "Now, friend, how much money have you?"

The knight's face grew red. "I have a few cents. It's all I have in the world. I, Sir Richard of the Lea, am a poor man."

"Do you give me your word this is true?"

"Yes. Look for yourself if you doubt it."

"No," said Robin. "I believe you. We take from the rich, but we do not harm the poor. Come, Sir Richard, cheer up. Come with us. Tell us your troubles. Maybe we can help you."

"I have troubles you cannot help, but I will go with you today." Sir Richard turned his horse. Robin and Will Scarlet walked on each side. After a while Robin spoke.

"I do not want to bother you," he said. "Do you want to tell us your troubles?"

"Why, Robin, I don't know why I should not tell you. I owed a lot of money. I had to pay. I borrowed the money on my castle and lands. In three days I must pay the money back. If I do not, I lose my castle and lands to the Chief Prior, the Bishop's right hand man. I will never get them back from him."

"Why did you waste your money so that you had to borrow?"

"I did not. I have a son, just twenty years old. Last year he became a knight.

As a new knight, he had to show how well he could fight. My wife and I were very proud of him. In the matches he won every fight he had. At last he had to ride against a great knight, Sir Walter. Even Sir Walter did not knock him from his horse. But a splinter from my boy's lance flew into Sir Walter's eye and killed him. Sir Walter had friends near the King. To save my boy from prison, I had to pay six hundred gold pounds. I might have raised the money, but the King laid more taxes on me. He took all my money away. So I had to get most of the money from the Prior. He made me put up my castle and lands for the money. The castle and lands are worth many times the money. I would not care, but it will kill my poor wife."

"Where is your son now?" asked Robin. He and Will had listened to every word.

"In the Holy Land," said Sir Richard. "He had to get out of the country."

"You have had bad luck," said Robin. "How much do you owe the Prior?"

"Four hundred gold pounds."

"What?" cried Robin. "They will take your castle and lands for only four hundred pounds? They are dirty robbers! What can you do if you lose your lands?"

"I do not care about myself. I would go to the wars in the Holy Land. But my wife's heart would break."

"Have you no friends to help?" asked Will Scarlet.

"They are afraid to help. I am now poor and have strong enemies."

Robin put his hand on Sir Richard's shoulder. "Don't worry," he said. "Maybe I can help you." Sir Richard smiled sadly, for he had little hope.

It was nearly dark when they got to Sherwood Forest. When still a way off from camp they could see that Little John and his men were already back. They, too, had brought somebody back. Robin laughed loud and long when he saw who it was — the Bishop of Hereford! The Bishop was walking up and down in an angry way. Three of his friars stood nearby. Six horses were tied to trees. Five were loaded down with big boxes. Robin walked over to the Bishop.

"What does this mean?" cried the Bishop. "Is this how you treat one so high in the church as I am? We were riding down the road. A great big fellow stepped out on the road. All these robbers came with him. This big fellow called me a fat pig and a church robber and made us come along."

"Was this the man?" asked Robin. He pointed to Little John.

"That's the man."

"Little John, did you call the Bishop a fat pig?"

"I did."

"And a church robber?"

"I did."

Robin turned to the Bishop. "He never tells lies," he said.

The men threw back their heads and laughed. The Bishop's face got red.

"Now, Bishop," said Robin, "we really are not bad men. Here everybody is the same. Here you are no Bishop. Take it easy and have a good time."

Robin's men now laid deer skins down for the Bishop and Sir Richard to sit on. They put up a mark. The men lined up for a shooting match. Shot after shot hit the mark. Never had Sir Richard or the Bishop seen such shooting. All the while Robin talked and joked with the Bishop and the knight. They soon forgot their own troubles. At last the Bishop spoke.

"I have never seen such good shooting before. But I have heard that you are the best of all. Show us how good you are."

"It is getting dark," said Robin, "but I will try."

He cut a thin branch and peeled off the bark. Then he marked off eighty yards. He pushed the branch into the ground and walked back. Allan-a-Dale handed him his bow. Robin picked out a good arrow. He fitted it, pulled the string to his ear, and let go. The men let out a loud shout. Will Stutely ran back with the branch. The arrow had split it in two. The men cheered again, for they were proud that Robin was the best shot in all England.

After more matches Allan-a-Dale got out his harp and sang. The silver moon rose over the trees. At last the men called that the dinner was ready. Robin led the Bishop and Sir Richard to where the food was spread. Talking and laughing they began to eat. When they had finished Robin stood up.

"I have a story to tell you," he said. "I want you all to listen."

He told them about Sir Richard's troubles — how he was to lose his castle and lands. The Bishop put away his wine. He looked down as Robin talked. The Bishop knew the story well. When Robin finished he looked at the Bishop.

"Do you not think that is bad for a churchman to do?" he asked. "Don't you think the Prior should be kind to others? Should he try to get land and castle from this knight?"

The Bishop said nothing.

"Well," said Robin, "you are the richest bishop in England. Will you not help this poor knight?"

The Bishop said nothing, nothing at all.

Robin turned to Little John. "You and Will Stutely go bring those horses here."

Will and Little John led the Bishop's horses back to Robin Hood. Robin took the list of goods from the friar who carried it. He handed it to Will Scarlet.

"Three rolls of silk for the town store keeper," read Will.

"We will not take any," said Robin. "He is a hard-working man." Robin's men took the silk and laid it aside.

"A roll of silk for the friars," read Will.

"They need no silk," said Robin. "But let them keep one-third. We sell one-third and give the money to the poor. One-third we keep."

"Wax candles for the church," read Will.

"Those they should keep," said Robin. "Read on."

And so Will Scarlet read through the list. Some things Robin let the Bishop keep. Of others he made three parts, as with the silk. At last Will came to the last line.

91

"The Bishop's box," he read finally.

The men brought the box to Robin. The Bishop's face grew pale.

"Have you the key?" asked Robin.

The Bishop shook his head.

"Open it with a sword," said Robin.

Will Scarlet got his big sword. He hit the box a mighty blow. It broke open. A great pile of gold fell out on the grass.

"Count it," said Robin.

Will and the others went to work. At last he said, "There are fifteen hundred gold pounds, master."

"Where does this money come from?" asked Robin.

"It is rent money from my lands," said the Bishop.

"Yes," said Robin, "taken from the poor. But I will not take it all. You may keep one-third. You can give us one-third. The other third goes to the poor."

Then Robin turned to Sir Richard of the Lea. "That good churchman, the Prior, wants to take your land. We can well use this church money to help you. You get

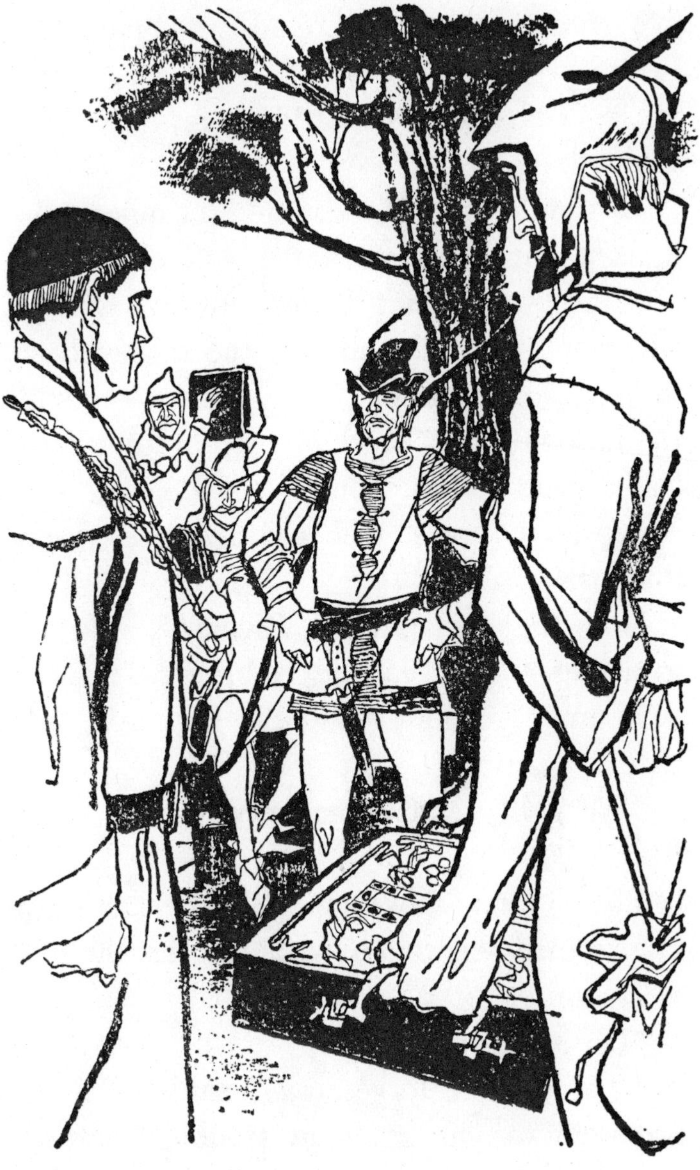

five hundred gold pounds to pay the Prior."

Sir Richard said nothing for a while. Then he spoke.

"I thank you, friend. But I cannot take it as a gift. This is what I will do. I will pay the Prior what I owe. In one year I will come back. I will pay the money back to you or the Bishop."

"I don't know why you want to pay it back," said Robin. "But if you do, you may bring it to us. I will use it more wisely than the Bishop."

Now the men put Sir Richard's gold into a bag. Others carried Robin's part away.

"I must go now," said Sir Richard. "My wife is waiting."

"We will send some men along," said Robin.

Little John spoke up. "Master, let me take some men to go with this knight and help him."

"Do so," said Robin.

"I will never forget this," said Sir Richard. "If you are ever in trouble, come to me. I will give my life for you." And Sir Richard and Little John and some of Robin's men started off through the forest.

"I must be going, too," said the Bishop. "It is getting late."

"Don't be in such a hurry," said Robin. "Sir Richard must pay his gold to the Prior in three days. I think you had better stay with us three days. You just might make some trouble for him. You can go hunting with us."

So the Bishop stayed. At the end of three days Robin let him go.

"I'll pay him back," said the Bishop. "Some day I'll pay him back for this!"

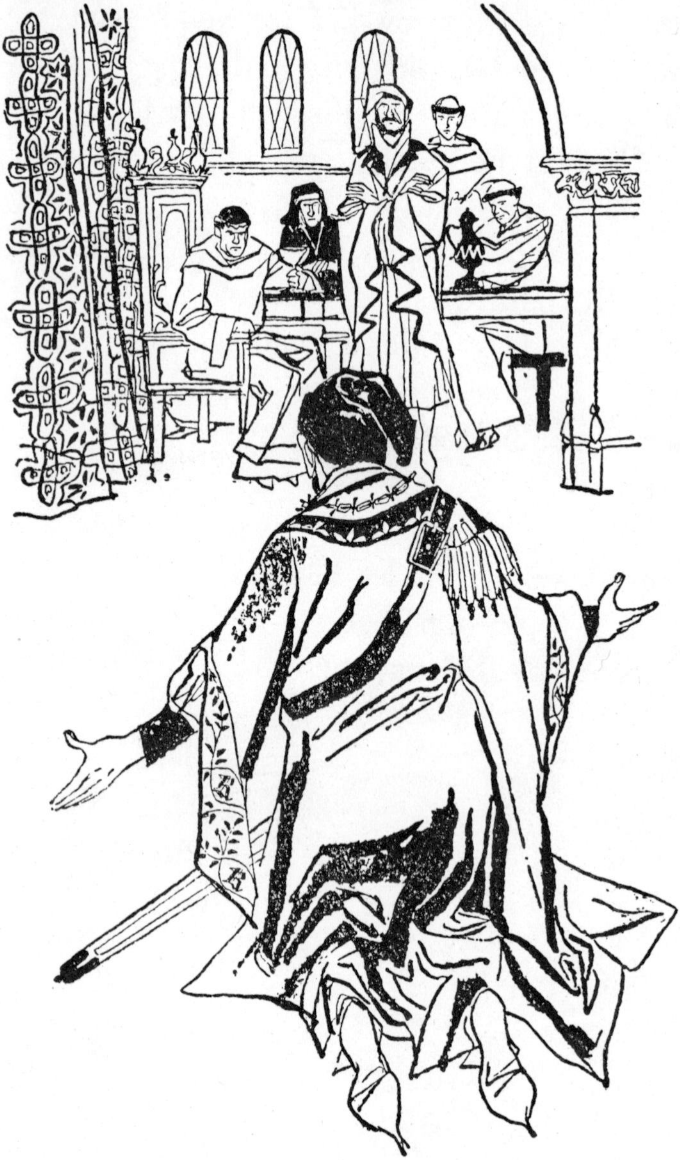

How Sir Richard of the Lea Paid What He Owed

Three days later a knight and a band of men came riding down the road. The knight wore a long gray robe. A sword hung from his broad leather belt. The knight was Sir Richard of the Lea. The band of men were Robin Hood's, led by Little John.

When they came to the castle where the Prior lived, Little John beat on the gate with his sword. An old man opened it.

"Where is your master?" asked Sir Richard.

"If you are Sir Richard of the Lea, he is waiting for you."

"I will go find him," the knight said.

Now while Sir Richard was riding, the Prior was having a fine dinner. The Prior himself sat at the head of the table. He was dressed in soft silk. A heavy gold chain hung from his neck. On his right sat Robin's old enemy, the Sheriff. On his left sat a lawyer. At the table sat other friars.

They were having a good time. The lawyer's old face was smiling. The Prior had already paid him eighty gold pounds. He had told the Prior how he could get Sir Richard's lands away from him. He had taken his money first because he did not trust the Prior.

"Are you sure you can get Sir Richard's lands, Prior?" asked the Sheriff.

The Prior took a long drink of wine. "Yes," he said. "I have been watching him. I know he has no money to pay me. He will have to give up his land and castle."

"That is right," said the old lawyer. "The Prior gets the land if he does not come to pay today. But don't forget, Prior. You must get him to sign that paper or he can make trouble later."

"Yes, I know," said the Prior. "This knight is so poor that he will gladly sign the paper for two hundred gold pounds."

"He has the finest land I ever saw," said a friar. "It is a shame that he must lose it for only four hundred gold pounds."

"That is enough from you," said the Prior angrily. "Mind your own **business.**"

"Never mind," said the lawyer. "I don't think he will even come today."

As the lawyer said this, they heard the sound of horses outside. The Prior told a friar to go to the window.

"I see about twenty men and a knight," he said. "They are coming in downstairs."

"Are you sure he will not make trouble?" asked the lawyer.

"Don't be afraid," said the Prior. "He will not hurt you."

The door now swung open. In came Sir Richard. His head hung low. His eyes were on the floor. His men stayed at the door. He came up to the Prior and went down on one knee. "Prior," he said, "you told me to come today."

"Have you my money?" said the Prior.

"I have not one penny on me," said Sir Richard. The Prior smiled happily. Sir Richard stayed on his knee.

"What do you want?" asked the Prior.

"I ask you not to take away my lands," said Sir Richard.

"If you have no money, you lose the land," said the lawyer.

"You are a lawyer," said Sir Richard. "Will you not help me?"

"No," said the lawyer. "The Prior gets the land."

"Will you not help me, Sheriff?" asked Sir Richard.

"Not I," said the Sheriff.

"Pay me four hundred pounds," said the Prior, "and you can keep the land."

"Will you give me another year to pay?"

"Not another day," said the Prior. "Pay up or give up the land and get out."

Then Sir Richard got to his feet. "A fine churchman you are!" he cried.

"Come," said the lawyer, "let us end this. Prior, what will you pay this knight to sign the paper that I have with me?"

"I would have given him two hundred gold pounds," said the Prior. "Since he talks as he has, he gets only a hundred."

"You won't get a bit of my land!" cried Sir Richard. He turned to his men. "Bring it," he called to Little John.

Little John handed him a leather bag. Sir Richard poured the gold on the table. "I owe only four hundred pounds. Here it is. You get not one penny more."

The Prior looked angrily at the gold. He had talked himself out of a hundred pounds. He had wasted eighty gold pounds on the lawyer. He turned to the lawyer.

"Give me back my money!" he cried.

"No, no!" cried the old man. "You get nothing back."

"Now, Prior," said Sir Richard. "I have paid you. I will get out of here."

The Sheriff was looking at Little John. "Robin Hood's right-hand man!" he said.

Little John smiled at the Sheriff. "Good-bye, Sheriff," he said. "I hope to see you soon — in Sherwood Forest."

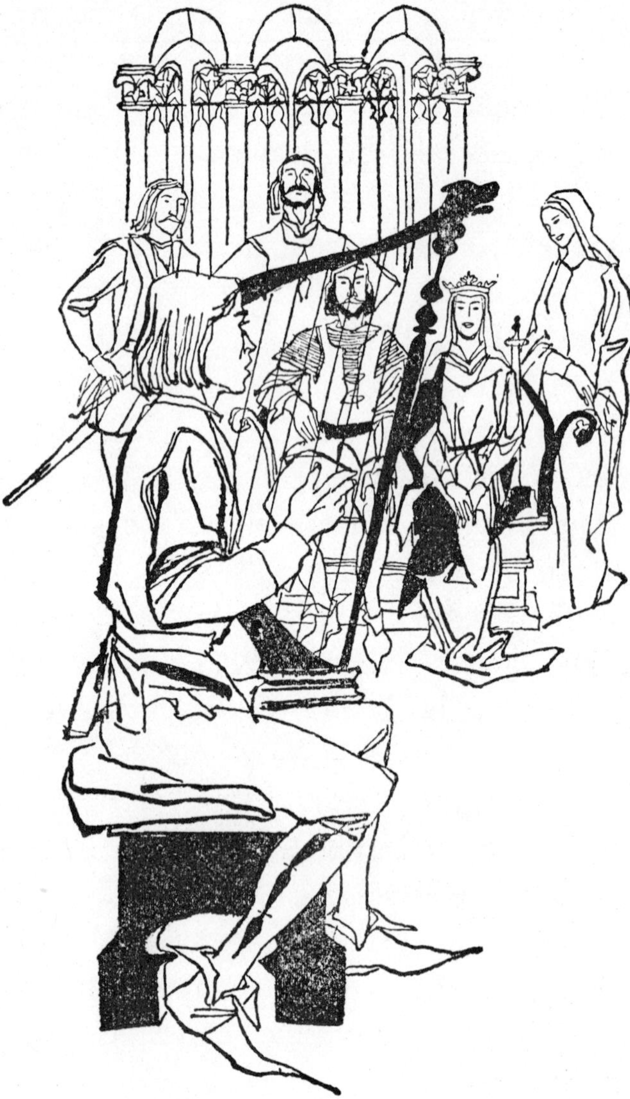

ROBIN HOOD
SHOOTS FOR THE QUEEN

The long dusty road stretched toward Sherwood Forest. A boy, about sixteen, came riding fast on a fine white horse. His clothes were silk and velvet. The people stopped to look at him. Some knew him. He was young Richard Partington, the Queen's page. He was riding from famous London Town to find Robin Hood.

Mile after mile he rode. At last he came to a little inn under some tall shade trees. Here he stopped. He called for a bottle of cool wine. Five big strong men sat before the inn — drinking beer. Two were dressed in Lincoln green.

The owner came out and handed the

wine to the boy, who stayed on his horse. Young Partington held up the bottle. "Here's to our Queen Elinor. May I soon find Robin Hood for her!" he said.

The two in Lincoln green began to whisper to each other. Then one, a great, tall fellow stood up. "What do you want with Robin Hood, boy? What does Queen Elinor want with him? We know him."

"If you do, I wish you would take me to him. The Queen wants me to talk to him."

"We know where to find him. But we will do nothing to make trouble for him. What does the Queen want?"

"Do not worry. I bring kind words to him from our Queen. Take me to him."

The two looked at each other. The tall one said, "I guess it is safe, Will." They both got up. "Come," he said.

The boy paid his bill and the three started down the road.

In Sherwood Forest Robin and his men lay under the trees. They listened as Allan-a-Dale played and sang for them. Suddenly they heard the sound of a horse's feet.

Soon Little John and Will Stutely came down the path through the trees. Between them rode Richard Partington, the Queen's page. Robin stood up. The boy jumped from his horse and went up to him.

"Welcome," said Robin. "Tell me what brings you to Sherwood Forest?"

"You must be the famous Robin Hood," said the boy. "And these must be your famous band of men. I bring you the words of Queen Elinor. She has heard much about you. She would like to see you. You are to come to London. She will see that you come to no harm and get back to Sherwood safely. In four days our good King Henry will hold a grand shooting match. All the famous bow men of England will be there. Our Queen would like to see you shoot against them. She sends you this golden ring. It comes from her own finger."

Robin took the ring and kissed it. He put it on his little finger.

"I will give up my life before I give up this ring," he said. "Boy, I will do as the Queen says. I will go with you to London."

"The Queen says you may bring some friends if you wish."

"I will pick three men," said Robin. "Little John, Will Scarlet, and Allan-a-Dale will go. Get ready, men. Will Stutely, you will take my place here."

Robin and the others hurried to get ready. Robin dressed himself in blue from head to toe. Little John and Will Scarlet wore Lincoln green. Allan-a-Dale dressed in red. Each man wore a steel coat under his other one.

For three days they rode toward London. At last they saw the towers and walls far away. They hurried on. Before long they found their way to the castle. When Queen Elinor heard they had come, she sent for them.

Robin Hood kneeled before her. "I am Robin Hood," he said. "You told me to come, so here I am. I will always do as you say even if it costs my life."

The Queen smiled and told Robin to get up. She sent for food. When they had eaten, she asked many questions about their life in Sherwood Forest. They told her many stories of what they had done. The Queen and her ladies laughed again and again to hear such wonderful stories. Then Allan-a-Dale sang for the Queen and her ladies. And so the time passed until the great shooting match.

The shooting match was to be in a big field. On the sides of the field were the tents of the men who would shoot. The King's men were formed into bands of eighty each. There were ten bands. Each band had its own tent. Over each colored tent flew a flag. Each band had its own flag. The yellow flag of one tent showed it belonged to the men of Tepus, the King's best captain. Gilbert of the White Hand was another famous captain. His flag was bright blue. Captain Clifton's flag was red.

A great crowd of people were to watch the shooting match. Men ran here and there. Boys sold food and drink. There were long rows of seats. The best place was kept for the King and Queen. People came from everywhere and began to fill the seats.

Ten targets stood at one end of the field. Each target had a colored flag, one for each band. The line was marked off from which the men would shoot.

At last came the sound of music. Six men rode across the field blowing silver horns. Behind them came King Henry on a beautiful horse. Queen Elinor rode at his side. Soldiers in steel armor marched behind them. After the soldiers came the people of the King's court.

The people rose and cheered. The King and Queen walked up the steps to their seats. When they had sat down, the horns blew again. Now the bow men came marching from the tents. A knight rode forward to call out the rules.

"Each man shoots seven arrows," he cried. "The three best men from each band will be chosen. These three each shoot three arrows. The best one from each band will be chosen. These ten men will shoot three more arrows each. The best shot wins first prize. There will also be a second prize and a third prize. The other seven men each get eighty silver pennies. First prize is fifty gold pounds, a silver and gold horn, and ten white arrows with golden tips. The second prize is a hundred deer from the King's forest. The second prize winner may shoot them when he wishes. Third prize is two great barrels of fine wine."

Now the shooting began. The captain of each band shot first. Then each man in the band had his turn. Arrow after arrow flew to the ten targets. At last the judges went to look at the targets. They called the names of the three from each band who had won. Ten fresh targets were put up. The shooting started again. Gilbert was one winner. Tepus and Clifton, too, won. The winners went to their tents to rest.

Queen Elinor turned to the King. "Do you think these are the best bow men in all England?" she asked.

"Yes," said the King. "They are not only the best in England. They are the best in the world."

"What would you say if I found three men better than your three winners?"

The King laughed. "You could not find three better men. Tepus, Gilbert, and Clifton are the best."

"I have three men to match against your three," said the Queen. "I will match them against yours this very day. But you must promise not to harm them."

Again the King laughed. "All right," he said. "Bring on your three men. I promise not to touch them for forty days. And if they can beat my three, they get the prizes. And just for some fun, will you bet on your men?"

"I know nothing about such things but, yes, I will."

The King could hardly stop laughing. "I bet ten great barrels of fine wine, ten barrels of beer, and two hundred sets of bows and arrows."

"All right," said the Queen. "So be it. I will put up these jewels I have with me."

"I agree," said the King. "Send for your men. Here come my ten men to shoot. I will match the three winners against your men."

Now the Queen whispered to young Richard Partington. The boy ran off into the crowd.

And now the ten winners took their places. The great crowd became quiet. Each man shot slowly and carefully. When the last arrow hit the target, the crowd shouted loud and long. Gilbert had three arrows in the white bull's eye. Tepus had two in the white and one in the next black ring. A captain named Hubert had beaten Clifton for third place. Gilbert's men shouted and cheered and shook hands with one another.

Now five men came walking across the field. The first was Richard Partington, whom all knew. But the others were strangers. One was dressed in blue, one in red, and two in Lincoln green. Three carried bows and arrows.

The King sent for Gilbert, Tepus, and Hubert. The people stopped cheering. They saw something was about to happen, but they did not know what it was. Some stood up to see better.

The four men kneeled before the Queen. King Henry looked hard at them. The Bishop of Hereford, sitting next to the King, knew the strangers well. He opened his mouth to say something to the King. He saw the Queen looking at him and closed his mouth. His face grew red. The Queen spoke.

"Locksley," she said, "I have bet the King that you can outshoot his men. Will you do it?"

"Yes, I will," said Robin Hood. "If I fail I will not shoot again."

"Who are these men?" asked the King.

"That fellow in blue is a robber named Robin Hood," cried the Bishop. "That big one is Little John. The other one in green is Will Scarlet. The one in red is called Allan-a-Dale."

The King looked angry. "Is this true?" he asked the Queen.

"Yes," said the Queen. "The Bishop ought to know them pretty well. Remember your promise."

"I will keep my promise," said the King.

"But after forty days this fellow had better watch out." He turned to his men. "Gilbert," he said, "if you three beat them I will fill your caps with silver pennies. If you lose, you lose your prizes to them. Do your best, boys. Go to it and beat them."

By now the crowd had heard the news. Everybody knew that the great Robin Hood was there. All stood up to see the famous outlaws.

Now six new targets went up, one for each man. Gilbert's team was to shoot first. Gilbert picked Hubert to start.

Hubert took his place. He fitted an arrow to his bow. He pulled the string back slowly. The arrow flew. Straight to the center it went. Again he shot. Again he hit the white bull's eye. His third shot just missed and landed in the black ring. The crowd shouted.

Robin Hood laughed. "Your turn, Will," he said. "You will have a hard time beating that."

Will Scarlet took his place. He tried too hard and lost his match on the first shot.

The arrow hit the next ring to the black. Robin bit his lip. "Will, Will," he said, "do not hold the string so long." Will shot twice more and hit the bull's eye both times. But Hubert had won. The people clapped their hands for Hubert.

"It looks as though you will lose," said the King. The Queen just smiled.

Now Tepus took his place. Like Will, he tried too hard. The first arrow hit the center ring, but the second hit the black. The third was another bull's eye.

"Little John," said Robin, "take your turn."

Little John shot three arrows without lowering his bow. One, two, three in the center! It was the best shooting of the day.

And now Gilbert took his place. He hit center with all three shots.

"Well done, Gilbert," cried Robin Hood. "You are a good shot." While he was still talking he let the first arrow fly. Almost without looking he shot the next two. The three arrows were so close together they looked like one. Never had the people seen such shooting. Gilbert took Robin's hand.

"You win," he said.

"No!" cried the King. "It's a tie. Let them shoot again."

"I will shoot all day if the King says so," said Robin. "Go on and shoot, Gilbert."

This time Gilbert's arrow hit the black ring. Robin again hit center. The King got up and left the field. Now all the bow men crowded around the winners. The judges brought the prizes. Robin won first prize; Little John, second, and Hubert, third.

"I will take the silver and gold horn," Robin said. "Gilbert, I give you the gold. You are a good man. To the ten captains I give the ten golden arrows."

Everybody cheered. Little John spoke.

"Tepus," he said, "I don't need the King's deer. I give them to you men."

Again the crowd shouted. Someone tapped Robin's arm. It was young Partington.

"The Queen says to run. The King is angry. He may break his promise."

"Thank you," said Robin. He called his men and they slipped away.

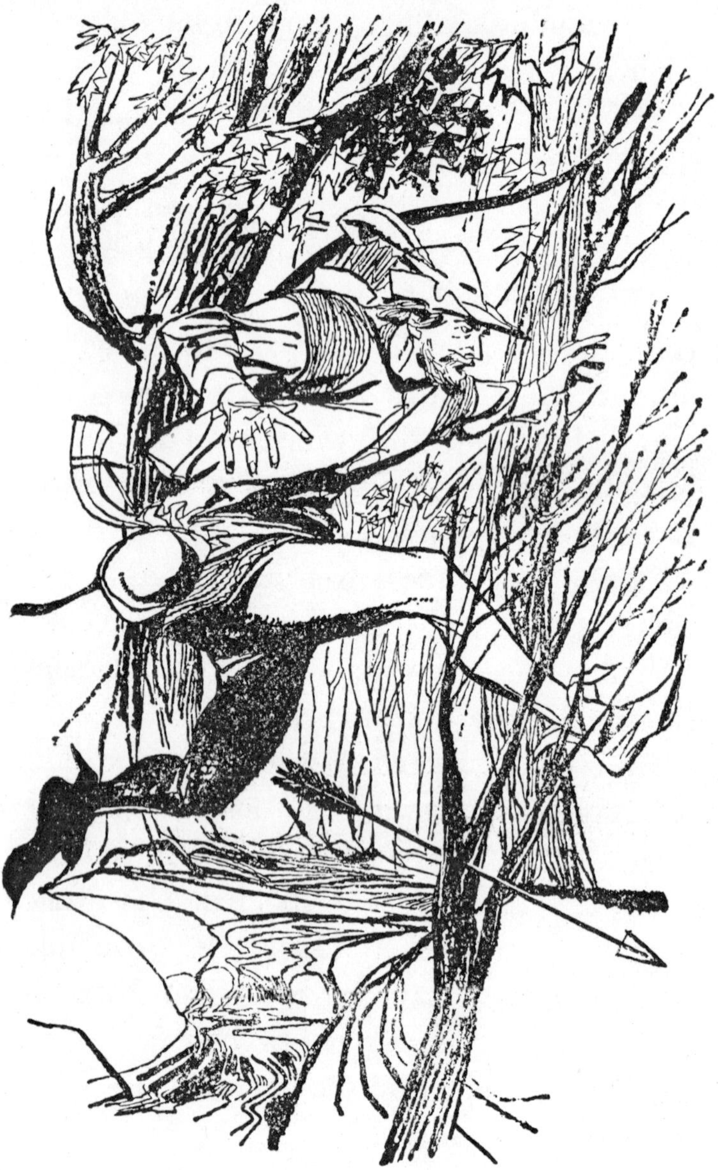

THE KING'S MEN CHASE ROBIN

Robin Hood and his men got away just in time. After they left, men went through the crowd looking for Robin.

When the King had left the field, the Bishop had gone with him. The King was angry. The Bishop was angry, too.

"It is too bad," he said, "that the outlaw should get away. If he gets to Sherwood Forest, you will never catch him."

"Is that so?" cried the King. "After forty days I will send men after him. I'll get him if I have to tear Sherwood Forest down."

"My lord, he will get into other forests. No, you must catch him now. If he gets away now, he will be free."

"What do you want me to do? You heard me promise the Queen not to harm him for forty days."

"You made the promise without thinking. Here is the greatest robber in England. The Queen does not know how bad he is. You can catch him. Forget your promise."

At last the King agreed. He sent his men after Robin. But one man told the Queen first. Then she sent the boy to warn Robin.

When night came, Robin, Little John, Will, and Allan came to a little inn.

"Let us stay here tonight," said Robin. "We are far from London and are safe. What do you say?"

"Sounds good to me," said Little John.

"I wish we were farther," said Will Scarlet. "If you think we are safe, let us stay."

They had a good supper. As they sat eating and drinking, the owner ran in to them.

"There is a boy outside," he said. "His name is Richard Partington. He wants to see the man in blue."

Robin went to the door. Richard was sitting on his fine white horse.

"What is it?" said Robin.

"The Bishop has set the King against you. Hundreds of the King's men are after you. They are to keep you from getting back to Sherwood Forest. Two bands of men are on this road, not far behind me. The Queen says to run, run, run!"

"Thank you, Richard," said Robin. "Tell the Queen I am on my way. I will make the owner here think we go to the next town. My men and I will go different ways to get back. Good-bye, good friend."

"Good luck," said Richard. He turned his horse back toward London. Robin went back into the inn.

"Up, men," he said. "They are after us. We go on to the next town." He paid the owner for their supper and they left.

When they could not be seen, Robin told them the news.

"You three turn east," he said. "I will turn west. We will not turn north to Sherwood until we get past the King's men.

Stay off the roads. Go through fields and forests." And so they shook hands and parted.

Not long after, a band of men rode up to the inn. They jumped from their horses and ran inside.

"They are gone," cried the captain. "Owner, where are they?"

"I heard them say they were going to the next town. Hurry, you may catch them on the road."

The King's men jumped on their horses and rode off.

Will, Little John, and Allan did as Robin had told them. Eight days later they were safely back to Sherwood. They had not met any of the King's men. But Robin was not back when they got home.

Robin had taken the harder way. Day after day he went on his way. When the Bishop heard that Robin had already gone from the inn, he hurried to help. He sent all the men to Sherwood Forest. He put men on every path and road which led to the forest. He took more men from the

Sheriff. The Sheriff saw his chance to get even with Robin. Will Scarlet, Little John, and Allan-a-Dale had slipped into the forest just before the roads were blocked.

Robin knew nothing of all this. He walked on through the fields toward home. He came to a little stream of water. He was thirsty, so he lay down to drink. On each side of the road were bushes and trees.

As Robin bent over to drink, something whistled past his ear. Quick as a flash Robin jumped over the stream and into the bushes. He knew an arrow had just missed him. As he landed, five or six more arrows flew after him. Up the road came the King's men. They jumped from their horses and ran into the bushes after Robin. But Robin was soon far down the road. The King's men were still beating the bushes.

Robin came to the top of a hill. Looking down, he saw another band of the King's men waiting for him. Robin turned and ran back. He turned left and outran the men. At last he sat down to rest. He was tired and very hungry.

As he sat resting, Robin saw a man coming down the road. Robin knew him. He was a foolish shoe maker who lived near Sherwood Forest. He had made a pair of shoes for a man and was now going back home. Robin's mouth watered. The shoemaker was carrying a fried chicken and a bottle of beer.

"Hello, friend," said Robin.

"Hello," said the simple shoe maker. "What are you doing there?"

"Why," said Robin, "I am waiting to catch golden birds. I put salt on their tails. But tell me, what have you there?"

"A chicken and some beer."

"Would you like to sell the chicken and beer? Look, I will give you my fine blue suit and ten silver pennies. You give me your old clothes, leather apron, and food. What do you say?"

"You are fooling me. My clothes are old. Yours are new and very pretty."

"I'll show you I mean it. Come, let us trade clothes. I will even give you some of the chicken and beer."

Robin took off his coat. When they had traded, Robin gave him the money. They sat down and soon the chicken and beer were gone.

Just as they finished, a band of the King's men came down the road. Before the two could move, the King's men had them. They knocked the shoe maker down and held him.

"Ha!" cried the captain. "We have you at last. We get the money for catching you! Don't say anything, Robin Hood. We know that blue suit too well."

The poor shoe maker did not know what to say. Robin tried to look as foolish as he could. "What do you want with this poor man?" he asked.

"Poor fellow?" cried the captain. "This is that famous robber, Robin Hood!"

They tied the shoe maker's hands and put a rope around his neck. Off they went to take him to the Bishop. Robin laughed until the tears rolled down his cheeks. He knew the Bishop would let the shoe maker go. He turned once more toward home.

But Robin was too tired to get to Sherwood Forest that night. As the sun was setting he came to an inn. The owner had three bedrooms, so Robin took one. He was so tired he took off his clothes and went to bed. He was asleep as soon as he lay down.

A little later a storm came up. Four men came in to stay for the night. The owner put two men each into the other two rooms. Soon they, too, were fast asleep.

Not long after, who should come in out of the storm but the Prior. He had his horse fed and sat down to eat. Then he asked the owner to give him a bed.

"I have four men in two beds now," said the owner. "There is only one other bed. A shoe maker is sleeping in it. You will have to sleep with him."

The Prior did not like that at all. Still, there was nothing else to do. He went up to the room. Soon he, too, was fast asleep.

And so the night passed. When the sun came up Robin awoke.

"Well," said Robin, "who can this be?" He looked at the man asleep next to him.

He began to smile. Quietly he got up. He put on the Prior's black robes. He slipped out the back door without waking anybody. The stable boy saw him coming.

"Do you want your horse, sir?" he asked.

"Yes, my son," said Robin. He got on the horse and rode toward Sherwood.

When the Prior awoke, he found his clothes, his horse, and his money were gone. He could do nothing but put on the shoe maker's clothes. When he had started home, he had more trouble. The Bishop's men caught him and tied him up.

"But I am the Prior!" he cried.

"Yes, we know," said the captain. "You fooled us yesterday and got away. We know you now, Robin Hood. The Bishop will be glad to see you!"

Robin rode down the road whistling. He passed the King's men but they did not even look at him. At last he came to Sherwood Forest. His men shouted and cheered when they saw him.

The Sheriff's men and the Bishop spent many days before they gave up.

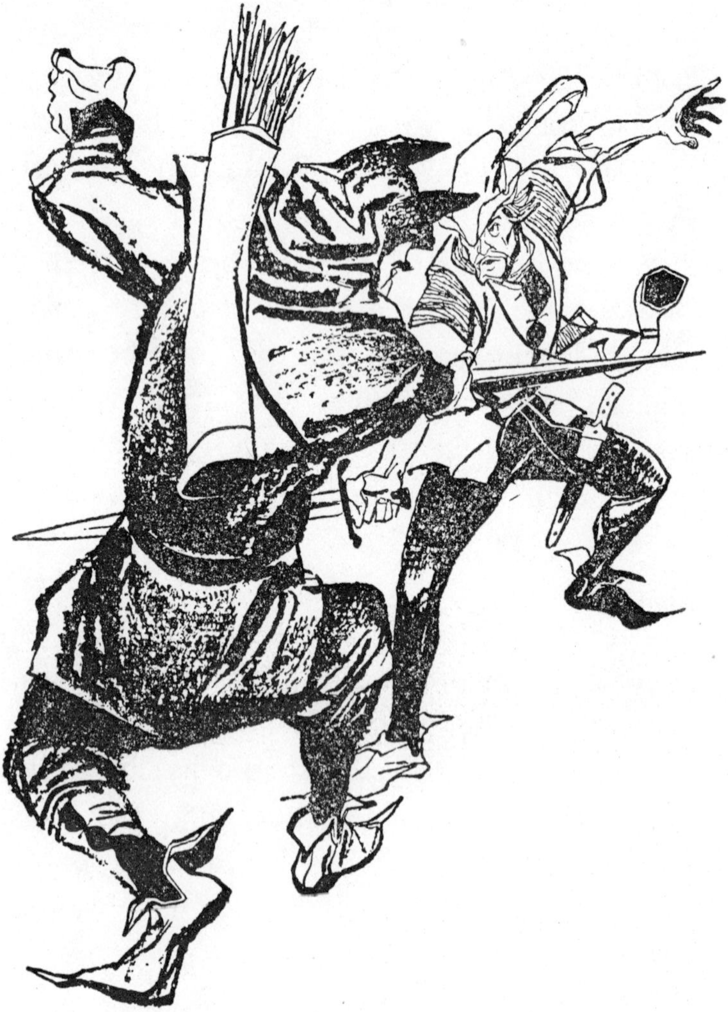

ROBIN HOOD FIGHTS GUY OF GISBORN

After the great shooting match Robin Hood stayed near Sherwood Forest a long time. During this time King Henry died and Richard became king. He was the King Richard who fought so bravely and was called the Lion Hearted.

One morning Robin Hood and Little John were walking through the forest.

"Let us each go his own way today," said Robin. "If I need you I will blow my horn. Maybe we can each find someone to bring home to supper."

So Little John went one way and Robin another. Robin went into the thickest part of the forest. Walking down a path, he came upon a stranger sitting under a tree. The man had not yet seen him, so Robin stood still. Never had he seen a man like him. From head to feet he was dressed in a horse's hide. Even the hat, which hung far over his face, was of the same leather. His legs were covered with the same hide. A heavy sword lay at his side. Near him lay a long sharp knife. His bow and arrows leaned against a tree.

"Hello, stranger," said Robin stepping forward. "Who are you? And what is that you are wearing? You're enough to scare a brave man."

The stranger said nothing, but pushed his hat back. Robin saw a dark cruel face with a hawk-like nose. He looked hard at Robin.

"Who are you, dog?" he said at last. His voice was hard and loud.

Robin laughed. "Don't be so fierce," he said.

"If you don't like my words, move on," said the stranger. "I'm as fierce as my words."

"Why, I do like your words, you pretty fellow," said Robin. He sat down and looked straight at the stranger.

The stranger looked back like a dog getting ready to bite. At last he said, "What is your name?"

"Maybe this, maybe that," said Robin. "You tell me yours. You are the stranger around here. Tell me, why do you wear those clothes?"

The other laughed. "You are as brave a man as I ever met. I don't know why I have not hit you. I wear these clothes to keep warm. I wear them because they are like steel against a sword blow. I don't care who knows my name. I am Guy of Gisborn. You have heard of me. I am the famous outlaw. The other day the Bishop sent for me. He said that if I would do something for the Sheriff here, he would get me a pardon and much gold. I went to see the Sheriff. He wanted me to find Robin Hood in Sherwood Forest. I am to bring him back dead or alive. So I am here to find him and kill him."

Robin had often heard of this outlaw. He grew angry to think the Sheriff would use such a man. But Robin kept on smiling.

"Yes," he said, "I have heard of you. I think this Robin Hood would like to meet you, too."

"The day he does, he will die."

"Oh, I don't know," said Robin. "Maybe he is a better man than you. I know him well. He is a good fighter."

"You may think he is good around here," said Guy. "But I know I can beat him. An outlaw! Why, I hear he killed a man but once. They say he is a great shot. I would not be afraid to shoot against him."

"Yes, they say he can shoot," said Robin, "but we are all pretty good around here with the bow. Now I'm not very good, but I would not be afraid to shoot against you."

"All right," said Guy of Gisborn. "Put up a target. I'll soon show you how to shoot."

Robin got up and broke off a thin branch. He peeled off the bark. Then he marked off eighty yards and stuck it in the ground. "There," he said, "let me see you split that branch."

Guy of Gisborn got to his feet. "What?" he cried. "The devil himself could not hit that."

"Maybe not," said Robin. "We can't tell until you try."

Guy shot twice. Neither time could he hit the branch. Robin laughed. "If you fight like you shoot, you will never beat Robin Hood," he said.

"Watch out, or I'll cut that tongue of yours out for you," said Guy.

Robin now took his turn. His arrow split the branch apart. Then he turned to the outlaw.

"There, you bloody dog!" he cried. "That shows how good you are. You have hurt enough people. You are ready to die. I am Robin Hood." Saying this, Robin pulled out his sword.

"You are Robin Hood? Now I am glad.

Say your prayers. You are going to die!" Guy picked up his sword.

Now came the fiercest fight anybody ever fought in Sherwood Forest. Each man knew it was a fight to the death. Soon Robin's sword began to get to Guy of Gisborn. Drops of blood flew to the grass.

At last Guy of Gisborn struck a fierce blow. Robin jumped back. As he did, he slipped and fell on his back. Guy gave a happy shout and swung his great sword. Robin put out his bare hand and caught the blow. The sword bit deep, but Robin hung on. He felt himself grow weak. Quickly he jumped up. He cut a swift blow at Guy's side. Guy dropped his sword. Like a flash, Robin ran him through. Guy screamed, turned, and fell on his face.

Robin wiped his sword and put it away. "This is the first man I have killed since I became an outlaw," said Robin. "But this man should die. The Sheriff sent him to kill me. I shall put on his clothes. Maybe I can fool the Sheriff. I ought to pay him back for this."

So Robin took off the bloody horsehide clothes from Guy of Gisborn. He picked up the other's sword and his own. He pulled the horsehide cap far over his face. Then he turned toward the Sheriff's town.

When Little John left Robin, he went the other way. After a while he came to a little house near the forest. He stopped. He thought he heard someone crying. The door was open, so Little John walked in. An old gray-haired woman sat in a chair crying.

Little John patted her shoulder. "Come," he said, "tell me your troubles. Maybe I can help you."

She shook her head sadly. "I have three fine sons. We are poor and were hungry. My oldest boy shot one of the King's deer so we could eat. The King's men tracked him here. They took all three sons to the Sheriff. The Sheriff says he will hang everyone who shoots the deer. The King's men are taking my boys to the Sheriff. He is staying at an inn, waiting for a man he sent to kill Robin Hood."

"Who is this man who is to kill Robin Hood? Well, let's try to save your sons first. Have you any old clothes here I can wear? If the Sheriff sees my Lincoln green suit, he will hang me, too."

The old woman had some clothes which her dead husband had worn. She got them out for Little John. He made some false hair and a beard out of wool. Then he put on an old tall hat. Sure that no one would know him, he took up his bow and headed for the inn.

The Sheriff and his men were waiting there for Guy of Gisborn to come back. To this inn came the King's men with the woman's three sons. They had to march into the room where the Sheriff sat.

"So!" cried the Sheriff when he had heard their story. "You will shoot the King's deer, will you? I'm tired of having the deer killed. You three will hang!" He turned to his men. "Take them out to those trees and hang them there."

The men led the three to the trees. Here they put ropes around their necks. They threw the ends of the ropes over the branch of a big tree. The three sons fell on their knees and begged the Sheriff to let them go.

The Sheriff just laughed. While this went on, Little John, dressed like an old man, came near. As the Sheriff was about to tell his men to pull the ropes tight, he saw him.

"Come here, old man," he said. "How would you like to make a little money?"

"Oh, I would like to," said Little John in a weak, old voice.

"Look," said the Sheriff. "Here are three fellows I must hang. My men don't like to do it themselves. String them up and I'll pay you. What do you say?"

"Why," said Little John, "I've never done anything like that. But, I can use the money. Have they said their prayers?"

"No," laughed the Sheriff. "You can hear them if you wish. But hurry."

So Little John went up to the three sons. He put his head close to the first as if he were listening to him pray.

"Stand still," he whispered. "I will cut the ropes. When I pull off this hat, run for the woods."

He cut the ropes. Then he went to the second and third sons and did the same. He did it so quickly that the Sheriff and his men did not see him do it.

Now he slipped an arrow into his bow. He pulled off his hat and false hair. "Run!" he cried. The three sons slipped from the ropes and ran into the forest.

"After them!" cried the Sheriff. "It is Little John — Robin Hood's man!"

But Little John had his bow ready. He cried. "The first man to move will die!"

The Sheriff's men stood still, for they knew Little John too well.

"After him, cowards!" cried the Sheriff. But not a man moved. Little John backed to the forest slowly. The Sheriff kicked his horse's sides. The horse jumped forward. As Little John pulled back the bow string to shoot, the bow cracked and broke. With a shout the Sheriff's men ran for him. Little John turned to run, but the Sheriff's horse was on him. The Sheriff swung his sword. The flat part caught Little John on his head. He fell to the ground senseless. The Sheriff's men jumped on him and tied his arms and legs.

"I'm glad I didn't kill him," said the Sheriff. "I want to hang him."

They threw Little John across a horse and rode back to the inn. The three sons had escaped, though.

Back at the inn, the Sheriff began to think. "I shall hang him tomorrow," he thought. "At last I'll get even with him. But wait — what if Robin Hood gets away from Guy of Gisborn? He will try to save Little John! He is brave enough, too. I'd better be sure and hang him now!"

So the Sheriff had his men take Little John back to the trees. As they rode, one of the Sheriff's men spoke up.

"Is that fellow down the road not Guy of Gisborn?"

The Sheriff looked. "It is! It is!" he cried. "He must have killed Robin Hood!"

When Little John heard this, the tears

started from his eyes. He could see the man's clothes were full of blood. Then he saw Robin's silver horn and sword.

"What luck?" called the Sheriff. "Your clothes are bloody!"

"Well, it's the blood of an outlaw. I killed him."

The Sheriff clapped his hands. "Guy of Gisborn, if you tell the truth, you will be well paid today."

"Is this not Robin Hood's sword?" said Robin, in Guy of Gisborn's voice. "Look, here is his bow. Here is his horn." Robin pulled the leather cap farther over his face.

The Sheriff laughed. "This is a happy day," he said. "Robin Hood is dead and I have Little John. Ask what you want, Guy of Gisborn. You shall have it."

"All right," said Robin. "I have killed the outlaw. Now let me kill his right-hand man."

"Take him," said the Sheriff.

"Men," said Robin, "put him over there against that tree. I'll show you how to stick a pig."

"Do as he says," called out the Sheriff. While they did so, Robin got his two bows ready. When Little John stood against the tree, Robin called out. "Get away, you men! Get back farther!" The men moved back. "Little John," whispered Robin, "it is I — Robin Hood. When I cut the ropes, take this bow. Now!" Robin cut the ropes. Little John jumped for the bow. Robin threw off the leather cap. "Stand back!" he cried to the Sheriff's men. "The first man to move dies!" He put his horn to his mouth and blew three times, loud and clear.

"Robin Hood!" cried the Sheriff. He turned and rode for his life. Little John let his arrow fly. When the Sheriff got home the arrow was still in his shoulder.

And so Robin Hood and Little John ran all the Sheriff's men home. When Will Stutely and Robin's men got there, their enemies were gone. They went back then to their safe Sherwood Forest. On the way they met the woman's three sons. They were glad to join the band.

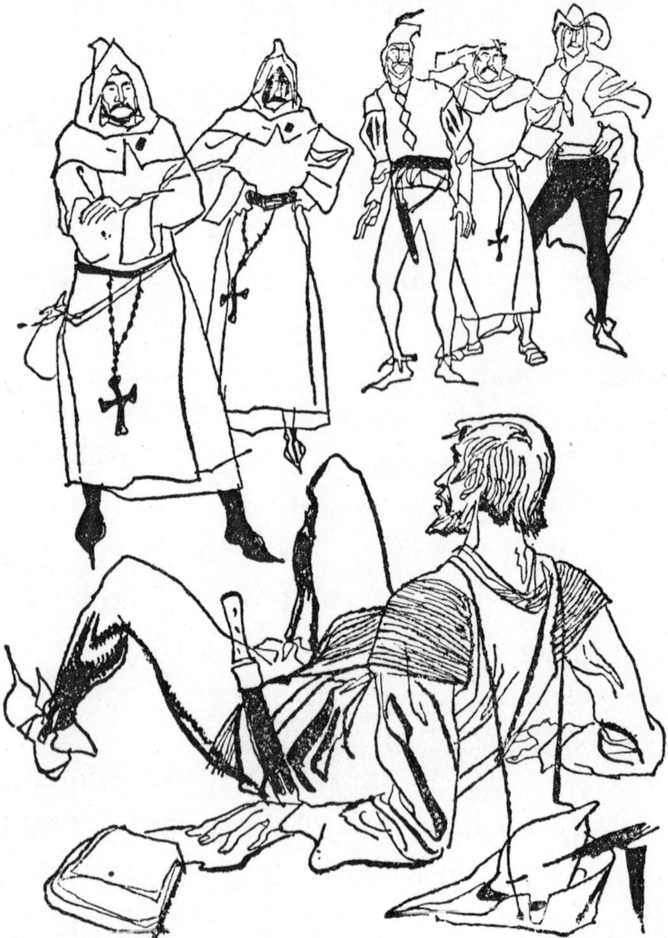

KING RICHARD
COMES TO SHERWOOD FOREST

All England was in a great stir. Their famous King Richard of the Lion's Heart was going from town to town. He wanted to see all parts of his land. The people wanted to see their King. At last he was to come near Sherwood Forest. The Sheriff and his men were busy getting ready for him.

Colored flags were hung from windows. The town hall was cleaned and painted. Men were building tables for a great dinner for the King. When the great day came, the people from miles around packed the streets. The Sheriff's men could hardly hold them back.

"Watch out whom you are pushing!" cried a church man in a long black robe. "Take care, or I will crack your head for you!"

The men dressed in Lincoln green gave a loud laugh. But one poked the friar.

"Shut up, Tuck," he said. "You promised not to make any trouble."

"All right," said Tuck. "But he doesn't have to step on my toes."

Just then came the sound of horns. The crowd pushed and looked down the street. A band of the King's men rode into sight. Each man was dressed in velvet and cloth of gold. Each carried a long silver horn. After these came a hundred knights in armor, two by two. The armor shone in the bright sun. Behind the knights came soldiers with spears and swords. Last came two riders. One was the Sheriff. The other was tall and wore a gold chain around his neck. His hair and beard looked like gold in the sun. He bowed left and right as he rode. The crowd shouted and waved as he passed. This was King Richard.

"Long live our good King Richard!" shouted a voice like thunder. King Richard looked to see a great strong friar waving his arm. The King laughed.

"Sheriff," he said, "you have the biggest and strongest friars here I have ever seen. I'd like to have an army of such men."

The Sheriff said nothing. His face was pale. He had seen that the man was Friar Tuck. He also saw the faces of Robin Hood, Little John, Will Scarlet, and Will Stutely in the crowd.

And so the King came. Nobody was more glad to see him than Robin Hood and his men.

That evening the great dinner was held in the town hall. At the head of the table sat King Richard. The Sheriff sat next to him.

"Sheriff," said the King, "I have heard much of a man called Robin Hood. He and his outlaws live in Sherwood Forest, I know. Can you tell me about them? I hear you have had a little trouble with them."

The Sheriff looked down at his plate.

The Bishop, who sat near, looked angry and bit his lip.

"I can tell little," said the Sheriff. "They are robbers and law breakers. They should all be hanged."

"I don't think so," said a young knight. "When the King and I were away in the Holy Land, I heard from my father, Sir Richard of the Lea. He wrote me about this Robin Hood. Let me tell you a story about him."

So young Sir Henry of the Lea, Sir Richard's son, told how Robin had helped his father. The King and the others laughed loud and long. The Bishop's face got red as an apple. Then others told more stories about Robin and his men.

Later that night King Richard sat with Sir Henry of the Lea and some of his friends. The King could not forget Robin Hood. "I would give a hundred gold pounds to meet this Robin Hood," he said. "I would like to see how he lives in Sherwood Forest."

"That is easy," said one. "For a hundred

gold pounds I'll see that you meet him."

"Good. How will you do it?"

"Why, let us dress in the robes of friars. Hang a bag with the gold under your robe. We will ride slowly through Sherwood Forest. I'll bet he will find us soon enough."

"I like your plan," laughed King Richard. "We will try it tomorrow."

So early next morning the Sheriff found them getting ready. "No, no!" he cried. "You must not do this! This fellow is an outlaw, a robber! He will not care if you are our King!"

"They tell me he has killed only Guy of Gisborn since he became an outlaw. All good men should thank him for that."

"Yes," said the Sheriff, "but —"

"Then why should I fear him? Would you like to go along?"

"No, no!" cried the Sheriff. "I never want to see that fellow!"

The King and his men now did as they had planned. They got on their mules and rode into the forest. They laughed and talked as they rode along.

"Say," called the King, "I am getting thirsty. We forgot to bring something to drink. I would give fifty gold pounds for a drink."

When the King spoke, a tall fellow in Lincoln green stepped into the path. He had a yellow beard and hair and merry blue eyes. He laid his hand on the King's mule.

"Why, holy brother," he said, "that is fair enough. For fifty gold pounds we will give you a drink of good wine. We will even give you something to eat, too."

He put a silver horn to his lips and blew. The bushes began to move. Before long, fifty men in Lincoln green were around the seven friars.

"Here, here!" said the King. "We are holy men. Who are you?"

"I am Robin Hood, holy brother."

"You let us go on our way."

"We couldn't do that," smiled Robin. "You are thirsty. I think you can pay for your drink, too. Let me see your gold. Or do you want me to take it?"

"Do not harm us. Here is the gold. We do not want your outlaw hands to touch us."

"My!" said Robin. "Who do you think you are, brother? The King of England? Here, Will. See how much he has."

Will Scarlet counted the money. "A hundred gold pounds," he said.

"Keep fifty. Put fifty back," said Robin. "There, brother. Take your part back. Now, let us look at your faces."

"We may not," said the King. "We seven agreed to cover our faces for twenty-four hours. Do not ask us to break our word."

"That I will not do," said Robin.

Now Robin and his men led the seven to their camp. Little John had taken sixty men with him that morning and was not back yet. Friar Tuck and about fifty men were at camp. King Richard looked at them.

"You have a fine band of men, Robin Hood," he said. "I think King Richard himself would be glad to have them."

"Sixty are away with Little John," said

Robin. "But you spoke of King Richard, friar. Every man here would die for King Richard. We are outlaws, but he is our King and we love him."

Friar Tuck came forward. "Well!" he cried. "Here are some holy men. I tell you, brother, I have a hard time here. I am the only holy man in this band." Everybody laughed.

"And who are you?" asked King Richard.

"See how good I am?" said Friar Tuck. "I do not even knock this fellow down. I am the good Friar Tuck, as you should know."

"Go, Tuck," said Robin, "and bring the wine. These men have paid already."

When Tuck brought the wine, Robin held up his cup. "Wait!" he cried. "Here's to our good King Richard. May he win over all his enemies."

They all drank, even the King himself. "Are you not an enemy of King Richard?" he asked. "You are an outlaw."

"No, we are not!" said Robin. "We

would give our lives for our King. Would you?"

The King laughed. "Maybe I would do more for King Richard than you. But I hear you men are the best shots in England. Will you show us how good you are?"

"Gladly," said Robin Hood. The men ran to put up a mark. "There is a good mark. Each man shoots three arrows. If any misses he gets a blow from Will Scarlet's fist."

David of Doncaster shot first and hit with all three. "Well done, David," cried Robin. "You have saved yourself a sore head."

Four or five others shot and hit the mark. Now and then one missed. The man had to face Will Scarlet then. Whack! One blow from Will's strong arm and the man rolled head over heels. King Richard laughed till the tears ran. Last of all Robin took his turn. His first two shots went straight to the center. "I would give anything to have this fellow fight for me," said the King to himself. Then Robin took his third shot. He did not see that the feather on the arrow was torn. It missed by an inch.

The men rolled on the ground and laughed. Never had they seen Robin miss the mark before. "It had a bad feather!" cried Robin.

"No, no, cousin," said Will Scarlet in his soft voice. "You made the rules yourself. Come close, I have something for you."

"Yes," said Friar Tuck. "You get your share."

"I made the rules, so I'll make this one," said Robin. "I'll take mine from this holy friar." Robin turned to the King. "Brother, will you give me the blow?"

"I should say I will," cried King Richard. "You took my fifty gold pounds. I owe you something for that. Get out of the way, boys. I shall roll him on the grass."

"You will?" said Robin. "If you knock me down I will give you your fifty pounds back. If you don't, I'll take your fifty."

"Good," said the King. He rolled up the

sleeve of his robe. The men whistled to see so big and strong an arm. Robin put his feet wide apart and smiled. The King pulled back his arm. Crack! The blow would have knocked a stone wall over. Robin rolled over and over and landed against a tree. Robin's men shouted and laughed till their sides hurt. Robin shook his head. At last he spoke.

"Will Scarlet," he said, "count out his fifty pounds. I should have let you hit me. I can still hear bells ringing."

The King laughed. But then all heard voices coming closer. Soon Little John and his band came running. With them was Robin's friend, Sir Richard of the Lea. Sir Richard called out to Robin.

"Hurry, my friend! King Richard is looking for you. Come to my castle and hide. Who are these strangers?"

"Why," said Robin, "these are holy men. This one just cost me fifty pounds and a sore head."

Sir Richard looked hard at the tall man in the black robe. Then he grew pale, for

151

he knew him. He dropped down on his knee before him. King Richard saw he was known. He threw off his head covering. Then they all knew him, for they had seen him in town. All fell to their knees.

"What is this, Sir Richard? Do you keep outlaws in your castle?"

"King Richard," said Sir Richard, "I owe my life and lands to Robin Hood. I must help him as he helped me."

Now one of the friars came forward. It was Sir Henry of the Lea, King Richard's friend, Sir Richard's son.

"You know that my father and I are your friends. I, too, would help Robin Hood. My father means you no harm."

King Richard began to smile. "Sir Richard, your son saved my life in the Holy Land. I shall do you no harm." Then the King turned to Robin Hood.

"You are an outlaw," he said, "but I like you. You are a good man and a brave man. I know you and your men love your king. I give you and your men free pardon. But you cannot stay here as outlaws.

Come to London with me. We will take Little John, too, and Will Scarlet and Allan-a-Dale. We will make your men King's foresters. They can care for Sherwood Forest. Now, let us have a great dinner."

So Robin's men sat down to eat together for the last time. Early next morning Robin and his friends set off with King Richard. Robin, Little John, Will, and Allan shook hands with all the band. They promised to come back often to see them. Then they rode away with the King.

This ends the Robin Hood stories. It was many years before Robin came back to Sherwood Forest. Robin became a great friend of King Richard. He fought in battle after battle with his King. The King made him captain of his bow men.

Little John came back and became a famous fighter. Will Scarlet was able to get back his castle and lands. Allan-a-Dale and his wife stayed with Robin and took care of his home for many years. Robin's men spent the rest of their lives as the King's foresters.